Flounder Fishing
Tactics and Techniques

By Keith Kaufman

ACKNOWLEDGEMENTS

I thank Lenny Rudow and Geared Up Publications for providing me the opportunity to write this book. My brother, Capt. Bruce Kaufman, used his outstanding artistic skills and his fishing knowledge to create the diagrams of flounder rigs that are included in this book. I also appreciate the knot diagrams provided by Take Me Fishing (Recreational Boating and Fishing Foundation.

I am very fortunate that for more than 10 years I had the opportunity to serve as Managing Editor of The Fisherman magazine, Mid-Atlantic Edition in Lewes, Delaware. Through that position, I was able to meet, fish with, and learn from expert anglers, many of whom have provided in-depth flounder fishing tips and tactics that are included in this book. They include Lenny Rudow, Andy Orr, Bob Baker, Pete Dressler and Claude Bain.

Chef David Haines has contributed scrumptious flounder recipes for our dining enjoyment. Tom Stauffer, Tom Pagliaroli and others have shared flounder photos that make this book more interesting and informative.

My father, Richard M. Kaufman, was an excellent writer and a voracious reader. He taught me that the best way to learn is to read. I appreciate that tremendous gift!

Finally, I express my sincere heart-felt appreciation for my Uncle Bill and my Uncle Harold. They took me fishing when I was young. They took the time and effort to show me how challenging and exhilarating it is to locate and catch fish. What I learned from them goes well beyond fishing. Bill Kaufman and Harold Hustedt are gone now and greatly missed. They shared their lives with me, and I am forever grateful.

GEARED UP PUBLICATIONS, LLC
EDGEWATER, MD
WWW.GEAREDUPPUBLICATIONS.COM

DEDICATION

To the wonderful women I have been so very fortunate to have had in my life: my wife Stephanie, my mother Evelyn, my mother-in-law Jean, and my aunts Marion and Irene. And to my favorite fishing companions, my sons Cody and Ross. Thank you for all of your love and support!

TABLE OF CONTENTS

CHAPTER 1

FLOUNDER FACTS, RECORD CATCHES, AND MANAGEMENT

Flounder inhabit the Atlantic Ocean and our inshore waters from Florida to Canada, and are most abundant from North Carolina to Massachusetts. From Delaware, Maryland and southward they're known as "flounder". Fishermen from New Jersey up through New England commonly refer to them as "fluke", or occasionally "summer

Fluke are flatfish, with both eyes on the same side of their head. They lie brown side up and camouflaged on the bottom, and ambush prey as it swims overhead.

flounder." No matter what moniker you hang on them, flounder are one of the most amazingly popular inshore species along our entire coast.

The army of recreational anglers that fishes for fluke each season pumps millions upon millions of dollars into the economies of many coastal locations. They support tens of thousands of east coast businesses, including charter boats and party boats, boat rental facilities, bait and tackle shops, restaurants, hotels... the list goes on and on. It's practically impossible to overstate the incredible importance of flounder, and flounder fishermen, to coastal communities.

Flat, brown on the top side and white on the bottom, with both eyes on the same side (brown side) of its head, fluke are one of the stranger-looking fish that we catch. They actually begin life much like other fish larvae, with one eye on each side of their head. However, after a few days, a baby summer flounder's right eye will start to slowly move, or migrate, over the top of the fish's head. It will eventually come to rest near the eye on the left side, or the brown side of the fluke.

It's weird looking, but it works. Fluke are ambush feeders. They lie on the bottom, brown side up, with both eyes constantly on the lookout for unsuspecting baitfish passing overhead. The top, brown side of a fluke is usually covered at least partially with sand or mud when the fish is hunting from its camouflaged position on the bottom, making them very difficult to see or detect. In addition, the coloration of their upper brown side changes (darkens or lightens) to more closely match the bottom, providing them with almost perfect concealment. When a baitfish swims overhead—unaware of the danger below—a fluke explodes off the bottom to grab the bait with its large, toothy mouth.

While flounder are ambush feeders, and spend the vast majority of their life on or very near the bottom, they are surprisingly quick swimmers and aggressive feeders. At times, they will chase baitfish to the surface and even attack them in a feeding blitz similar to that of other predators commonly seen breaking water.

Since the eye that moves ends up on the left side of the fish, summer flounder are in a group of flatfish called "left eye" flounder. The scientific name for fluke is Paralichthys dentatus. The winter flounder is a totally different fish–a "right eye" fish–with both eyes on the right side of its head.

In addition to predator, flounder are also prey. Big bluefish, striped bass, shark, and others at the top of the food chain will attack and eat flounder. In years past, when chopper bluefish blitzed the surf along North Carolina's Outer Banks each fall, they would chase flounder, speckled trout and other species right up onto the beach. It was possible to walk down the beach and pick up flounder and trout that swam ashore in attempts to avoid gator blues and their menacing jaws of death.

There are a number of factors about fluke that compel so many anglers to pursue them with relentless enthusiasm and determination. They include the delicious meals they provide, and how easily accessible they are, even during broad daylight in the heat of summer (when many other fish will only bite at the crack of dawn, late in the evening, and at night).

Fluke are an incredibly popular item on restaurant menus. Whether ordered in a restaurant or prepared at home, fluke fillets are a special treat at any seafood lover's dinner table. In fact, you don't even have to be a fish fanatic to enjoy white, mild, flaky fluke fillets. And, in chapter 9, Chef David Haines will provide us with scrumptious fluke recipes for our dining enjoyment.

The availability of fluke at easy to reach locations up and down the coast also adds to their appeal. Plenty of fluke are caught each season by anglers who aren't even in a boat. Anglers on beaches, piers, docks and bridges very often find flounder right at their feet. In fact, I have seen good surf fishermen walk into the water until they're in about thigh deep, and then turn around, face the sand, and fish the very narrow stretch of water between them and the beach!

Lots of fluke are caught each season by anglers in small, 14 and 16 foot aluminum and wooden boats that don't break the family budget to own. And even if boat ownership is out of the question, small skiffs like these are quite often available for rent in marinas near flounder hotspots, and are inexpensive to rent. They're perfect for drifting back bays, tidal creeks and canals, which are often very productive locations. Especially in the spring, particularly during the first of an outgoing tide in the late afternoon, you need no more than a small boat like this to catch your fair share of flounder. During flood tide, the high sun will have warmed the shallow water, attracting bait-fish, which means hungry fluke aren't far behind. The warm, outgo-ing water will pull baitfish out of the shallows, triggering a good fluke bite.

Outstanding fluke fishing at easily-accessible near-shore and on-shore locations are a big part of the fluke fishing attraction. It doesn't cost much to fish these locations, and it's possible to take the

Flounder provide lots of fishing fun for the entire family!

entire family for a few hours of quick, easy and productive fishing fun. Public bridges, piers, beaches, and waterfront parks offer great opportunity—and the keeper-size fish you catch will make tasty meals! But, on the other hand, fluke also frequent deeper-water shoals, drop-offs, lighthouse rockpiles, wrecks, and reefs, where bigger, sturdier boats with quality electronics and in-depth boating and fishing skills are required to locate and catch them. These areas provide different challenges, which result in a sense of personal satisfaction that many fishermen find very rewarding. What it boils down to is that fluke offer exciting fishing opportunities for anglers of all types.

Flounder spawn in September, October and November, as they migrate to the offshore grounds deep in the ocean, where they spend the winter. Spawning usually takes place in water that's 53 to 66 degrees and 60 to 160 feet deep. A single fish can release hundreds of thousands of eggs, while bigger female flounder release several million eggs. The eggs float in the water and hatch in about three days. When they first hatch, fluke have eyes on both sides of their head, just like most other fish. But then, one eye begins that remarkable journey around the fish's head.

Drifting, the migrating larvae move inshore and grow quite quickly. When it's a year old, a fluke is usually 10" to a foot long. Most of the fluke length/weight charts I have seen say a fluke hits about one pound in weight when it grows to 15" in length. Following are approximate weights for fluke of various lengths:

15 to 16 inches	1 to 1-1/4 pounds
17 to 18 inches	2 to 2-3/4 pounds
19 to 22 inches	3 to 4 pounds
23 to 26 inches	5 to 7 pounds
27 to 29 inches	8 to 9 pounds
30 inches	10 pounds
37 inches	20 pounds

Fluke migrate offshore each fall so they can pass the winter months in water that can be as much as 500 feet deep. Fluke

Flounder winter on the offshore grounds, then migrate inshore to coastal areas in March, April and May.

migrate back to the coastal areas, and into bays and sounds, during the months of March, April, and May, depending on location and water temperatures. Fluke prefer water temperatures between 65 and 80 degrees. They stay inshore until October, when cooling water and decreasing daylight prompt then to head offshore again. By their third year, fluke are sexually mature and will spawn for the first time.

In its third year of life, a flounder will be about 15 inches long, and weigh just less than two pounds. Many, many of the fluke caught each season are one to three pounders. Most anglers would consider a five to eight pound fluke to be a real nice catch, while any fish over 10 pounds is a bragging-size, trophy doormat! Flounder can grow to 30 inches or more in length, and weigh up to 20 pounds, although super-sized fish like that are a truly remarkable catch.

RECORD BOOK FLUKE

Record fluke catches, as of early 2007 when this book was written, are as follows:

International Game Fishing Association All-Tackle Record: The IGFA All-Tackle World Record is a behemoth 22 pound, seven ounce barn-door fluke caught by Charlie Nappi in New York on September 15, 1975. He was using a live snapper bluefish as bait.

Connecticut: The Connecticut state record fluke is a 14 pound, four ounce doormat caught in 2006 by Quinto Fillippino at Fayerweather Island.

Rhode Island: The Rhode Island record was set way back in 1962, when G. Farmer nailed a huge 17 pound, eight ounce fluke in the Narrow River.

Massachusetts: An immense 21 pound, eight ounce fluke holds the Massachusetts state record. It was caught by Joseph Czapiga at Normans Island on September 25, 1980.

New York: The New York state record is Charlie Nappi's IGFA All-Tackle World Record 22 pound, seven ounce fluke.

New Jersey: The New Jersey state record has been on the books for more than 50 years! It was in 1953 when Walter Lubin laid claim to the record with a dandy 19 pound, 12 ounce fluke.

Delaware: William Kendall was fishing Delaware's Indian River Inlet on October 7, 1974, when he caught Delaware's biggest flounder, a huge 17 pound, 15 ounce fish.

Maryland: Maryland recognizes two state record flounder, one for flatfish caught in the Chesapeake Bay and the other for those caught along the Atlantic Coast. The Chesapeake record, at 15 pounds, was caught on October 14, 1978 by Kenneth Grimes, at buoy 50.

Maryland's Atlantic coastal record is a fine 17 pounder hooked on October 3, 1974 at Assateague Island by Anthony Vacari.

Virginia: The Virginia state record has been on the books for nearly four decades! The 17 pound, eight ounce doormat was caught on July 22, 1971 by Charles Cross while he was fishing cut bait in Baltimore Channel. Claude Bain, Director of the Virginia Saltwater Fishing Tournament, believes this is a record that could very well be surpassed within the next several years. In 2006, anglers in Virginia registered a staggering 78 flounder that weighed 10 pounds or more! With big fish so abundant, it would be no surprise if a new record-setter is caught soon.

North Carolina: The North Carolina record is a huge 20 pound, eight ounce super-sized flounder that Harold Auten caught at Carolina Beach in 1980.

In this information about state and IGFA records, one point jumps out: September and October are prime times to fish for trophy fluke.

Good luck in your quest for a record book fluke—obviously, the more you know about fluke and fluke fishing, the better your chances of catching a huge fish, one that's heavy enough to put you in the record books. But one of the great things about fishing is that anyone, even someone brand new to fishing, might just get lucky enough to hook up with a record-breaking flounder. Good luck!

FLUKE MANAGEMENT

Both the recreational fluke fishery and the commercial fishery are managed under a coast-wide management plan. After many years of regulating fisheries on a state-by-state basis, the authorities determined that looking at fish populations as a whole, up and down the coast, was a far more effective method of management. The recreational harvest is controlled by size limits, daily possession limits, and/or closed seasons. The commercial harvest is controlled by gear restrictions, size limits and landing quotas.

Because fluke are one of the most important, valuable species along the entire East Coast for both recreational fishermen and commercial watermen, fluke management and regulations are incredibly controversial. As this book was written in early 2007, the issues of fluke management, regulations, and stock biomass rebuilding were absolutely white-hot. Some people say last-minute action by Congress and President George W. Bush "saved" the 2007 recreational fluke season, although there are plenty of people who say the season wasn't "saved" at all. They believe what was received was too little, too late. They're convinced the required reduction in the fluke harvest, and what they consider to be inept and improper fluke management, are destroying recreational fluke fishing and the many East Coast businesses that are dependant on a strong, vibrant fluke fishery. It won't end in 2007—fluke management will be an extremely contentious issue for many years to come.

It has been mandated that the biomass stock of flounder must be rebuilt to 204 million pounds. At first, the year that goal had to be reached was 2010. According to the National Marine Fisheries Service (NMFS,) for a 75-percent chance of reaching that goal by 2010, the 2007 total allowable landings (TAL) of fluke could be no more than 12.98 million pounds. Total allowable landings of 12.98 million pounds would have required states to cut their 2007 flounder landings by 50 percent to 75 percent over what was allowed in 2006. Recreational anglers, the businesses that depend on them, and many other interested parties went ballistic. That huge cut would

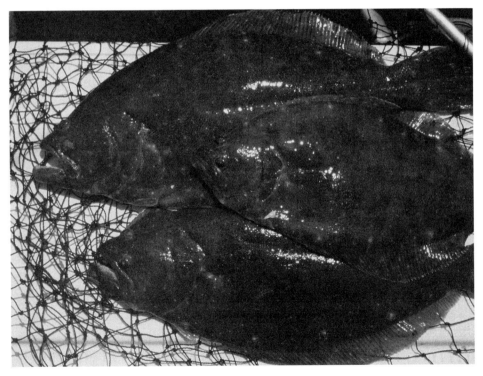

Flounder management, and the size and possession limits that are established in each state every year, are always controversial issues.

have been devastating to anglers and many fluke-related businesses like bait and tackle shops, charter boats, party boats, and rental boat facilities.

As the emotional uproar raged, a compromise was reached. The Magnuson-Stevens Fishery Conservation and Management Act that was approved by Congress and signed into law by the president in early 2007 included a three-year extension to the timeframe for rebuilding the flounder stock biomass. Instead of 2010, the Act allows the targeted biomass goal of 204 million pounds to be reached by 2013. The Recreational Fishing Alliance (RFA) was a driving force behind the extension to the timeframe. That meant more fluke could be allocated to each of the states, and the reduction in the total allowable landings for 2007 would not have to be quite so drastic.

Instead of 12.98 million pounds for 2007, the states received 17.11 million pounds. At 17.11 million pounds, landings will still have to be reduced by 27 percent; some states will be required to make further cuts to their recreational size limits and possession limits based on going over quota in 2006. As an example, Virginia has had to make deep cuts. The minimum size limit in Virginia for 2007 is 18-1/2 inches–that's two inches more than the 2006 size limit on flounder. And, at the same time the possession limit dropped from six fish in 2006 to five fish in 2007. On top of these hits, for the first time in two years Virginia also has flounder fishing closures in 2007 from January 1 to March 31, and from July 23 to July 28. Is it any wonder why fluke management and regulations are such highly combustible issues?

Forty percent of the 17.11 million pound TAL goes to recreational anglers, while 60 percent goes to the commercial industry. That also rankles many, many recreational anglers, as historically, the fluke fishery was primarily recreational.

For the extension to 2013 to remain in place, there cannot be over-fishing of fluke, there must be a mechanism in place that ensures over-fishing does not occur, and the fluke stock biomass levels must continue to increase.

In state waters, which are from the beach to three miles out (including bays and tidal rivers), flounder are managed by the Atlantic States Marine Fisheries Commission (ASMFC), and each particular state's fish and game division. In federal waters from three to 200 miles offshore (the Exclusive Economic Zone or EEZ), flounder are managed by the Fishery Management Councils of the United States

**Fluke management and regulations are
contentious issues, affecting every flatfish
lover on the coast.**

Department of Commerce. Fluke are managed under a federal management plan (FMP) developed by the Mid Atlantic Fishery Management Council and the Atlantic States Marine Fisheries Commission (ASMFC).

The ASMFC coordinates the conservation and management of summer flounder and other near-shore marine fisheries and resources, in states all along the Atlantic coast. A total of 15 coastal states from Maine to Florida, also including Pennsylvania, are represented on the Atlantic States Marine Fisheries Commission. Each state on the commission is represented by three commissioners.

The rules and regulations promulgated by the ASMFC are too numerous and constantly changing to list here, but you can read the management plans, news releases, stock status, and other information from the Atlantic States Marine Fisheries Commission at its website: http://www.asmfc.org/. Or, call the ASMFC in Washington D.C. at (202) 289-6051.

The Mid Atlantic Fishery Management Council is responsible for management of fisheries in federal waters (three to 200 miles) off the Mid Atlantic coast. States with voting representation on the council include New York, New Jersey, Delaware, Maryland, Virginia, North Carolina and Pennsylvania.

The Mid Atlantic Fishery Management Council established the original Federal Management Plan for flounder in 1988. Since 1991, 13 amendments have been approved, and they include establishing recreational harvest and size limits, commercial quotas, and establishing region-specific conservation equivalency measures for summer flounder.

Again, the rules and regulations published by the Council are prolific and ever-changing, and to find out more about them, you can log onto the website for the Mid Atlantic Fishery Management Council at http://www.mafmc.org/mid-atlantic/mafmc.htm. Or, call the Mid Atlantic Fishery Management Council in Dover, Delaware, at (302) 674-2331.

If the ASMFC and the Mid Atlantic Fishery Management Council web sites leave you hungry for more, you can also check out the

National Marine Fisheries Service website, where you'll read about the National Oceanographic and Atmospheric Administration. Here, we learn that NOAA's National Marine Fisheries Service is the federal agency, a division of the Department of Commerce, responsible for the stewardship of the nation's living marine resources and their habitat. NOAA's National Marine Fisheries Service is responsible for the management, conservation and protection of living marine resources within the United States' Exclusive Economic Zone (water three to 200 mile offshore). Using the tools provided by the Magnuson-Stevens Act, NOAA's National Marine Fisheries Service assesses and predicts the status of fish stocks, ensures compliance with fisheries regulations and works to reduce wasteful fishing practices. Care to learn more? The National Marine Fisheries Service website is http://www.nmfs.noaa.gov/.

FLOUNDER REGULATIONS

Constantly subject to change, the 2007 flounder regulations (where available at press time) I am including could very well be obsolete by the time you read them. So, why include the always-evolving regulations in this book? I thought it would be a good idea to also provide them as a point of reference, along with the website addresses you can use to access up-to-date, current regulations. In addition, many of these websites also contain information about any necessary fishing licenses and boat stamps, links for marine weather forecasts, buoy reports, tidal information, sunrise and sunset times, lists of public boat ramps, charts, suggested fishing hot spots, and other information of great value to flounder fishermen. Remember—these rules are constantly changing. DO NOT read them here, and accept them as current. They are merely stating what the rules were at the time of this writing, along with contact information you can use to obtain the current regulations for each state, for your use as a reference.

Minimum size limits are increasing, up to 17, 17-1/2, and even 18-1/2 inches in some states.

MASSACHUSETTS:

The homepage for the Massachusetts Division of Marine Fisheries is http://www.mass.gov/dfwele/dmf/index.html.

For fishing regulations, visit http://www.mass.gov/dfwele/dmf/recre ationalfishing/rec_index.htm#finfish.

For 2007, Massachusetts established a 17-1/2 inch size limit, with a seven fish per person per day possession limit, with no closed season, on fluke. The phone number for the Division of Marine Fisheries is (617) 626-1520.

RHODE ISLAND:

The web address for the State of Rhode Island Department of Environmental Management is http://www.dem.ri.gov/index.htm.

Rhode Island fishing regulations are at http://www.dem.ri.gov/pro grams/bnatres/fishwild/mfsizes.htm.

The phone number for the State of Rhode Island Department of Environmental Management is (401) 222-6800. Rhode Island fluke regulations had still not been established by the time this book went was published—providing yet another example of how these rules can change from one day to another. Make sure you've checked them out lately before you go fishing, regardless of what state you're in.

CONNECTICUT:

You'll find the Connecticut Department of Environmental Protection at http://www.ct.gov/dep/site/default.asp.

Check out Connecticut fishing regulations at http://www.ct.gov/dep/cwp/view.asp?a=2696&q=322740&depNav_GID=1647.

The Connecticut Department of Environmental Protection phone number is (860) 424-3000. For 2007, Connecticut has established an 18 inch size limit, with a daily possession limit of six fish per angler. The 2007 fluke season is April 30 to December 31.

NEW YORK:

Here is the website for the New York State Department of Environmental Conservation: http://www.dec.state.ny.us/index.html.

New York fishing regulations are at http://www.dec.state.ny.us/web site/dfwmr/marine/finfish/swflaws.html.

Dial (518) 402-8920 for Fish, Wildlife and Marine Resources. For 2007, fluke regulations in New York feature an 18 inch minimum size limit, a four fish per angler daily possession limit, and an open season of May 6 to September 12, 2007.

NEW JERSEY:

The homepage for the New Jersey Division of Fish and Wildlife is http://www.njfishandwildlife.com/index.htm.

New Jersey saltwater fishing regulations are available at http://www. njfishandwildlife.com/njregs.htm#fishing.

For more information, call (609) 777-DEP3 (3373). For 2007, New Jersey has established a 17 inch size limit, with an eight fish daily possession limit per angler. The 2007 fluke season is May 26 to September 10.

DELAWARE:

The Delaware Division of Fish and Wildlife can be visited at: http:// www.fw.delaware.gov/FWPortal.htm.

For Delaware fishing regulations, visit http://www.fw.delaware.gov/ Fisheries/FishingInfo.htm.

For more information, call 1 (800) 523-3336. Like Rhode Island, Delaware's 2007 flounder regulations had still not yet been established when this book was printed.

MARYLAND:
The homepage for the Maryland Department of Natural Resources is http://www.dnr.state.md.us/sw_index_flash.asp.

The following links provide fishing regulations and other important information for both Maryland's portion of Chesapeake Bay, and Maryland's Atlantic coast and coastal bays. Because of the nature of flounder's migration patterns, those caught in the in the Maryland portion of the Chesapeake Bay are rarely as large as those caught along the Atlantic Coast. To provide middle and upper Chesapeake Bay anglers with the opportunity to still fish for fluke, this area has differing regulations. They can be found at:

http://www.dnr.state.md.us/fisheries/regulations/recregchrt.html.
http://www.dnr.maryland.gov/fisheries/regulations/coastalbaysreg ulations.html.

In Maryland's portion of Chesapeake Bay in 2007, flounder season is open year round with a 15 inch size limit and two fish per person per day possession limit. Along Maryland's Atlantic coast, the size limit for 2007 is 15-1/2 inches, the season is open year round, and the possession limit is four fish per day.

Here's another good Maryland website: http://www.dnr.state.md.us/ fisheries/regulations/regindex.html.

Phone numbers for the Maryland Department of Natural Resources are 1 (877) 620-8DNR (8367), while out-of-state residents can dial (410) 260-8367.

VIRGINIA:
The homepage for the Virginia Marine Resources Commission is http://www.mrc.virginia.gov/.

The fishing regulations for Virginia tidal waters (except the Potomac River) can be found at http://www.mrc.virginia.gov/regulations/swre cfishingrules.shtm.

To call the Virginia Marine Resources Commission Main Office, dial (757) 247-2200. For 2007, Virginia established an 18-1/2-inch size limit, with a five fish daily possession limit per angler. In 2007, Virginia established closed seasons of January 1 to March 31, and July 23 through July 28 (it is illegal to possess flounder of any size during those time periods).

The Potomac River, which is shared by both Virginia and Maryland, has its own set of fishing regulations. For Potomac River fluke fishing information, visit http://www.prfc.state.va.us/sports/sport_fishing_blue_sheet_2006.htm.

NORTH CAROLINA:
The North Carolina Marine Fisheries Division is at http://www.ncdmf.net/.

Fishing regulations can be found at http://www.ncdmf.net/recreation al/recguide.htm.

The phone number for the North Carolina Marine Fisheries Division is (800) 682-2632, or (252) 726-7021. In 2007, flounder regulations for North Carolina's ocean waters are a 14-1/2 inch minimum, with an eight fish daily possession limit per angler. In North Carolina's inland waters, the flounder size limit is 14 inches and the daily possession limit is eight fish.

After glancing at these regulations, one may well wonder why there was such a huge disparity in minimum size and bag limits from state to state. Why, for example, should Maryland have a 15-1/2 inch minimum size while Virginia's limit is 18-1/2 inches? You must remember that each state had to cut its individual harvest based on what it had caught in prior years. Virginia's minimum size limit is only so high because this state is so rich in high quality flounder waters—and it enjoyed such a strong angling effort—that it vastly over-caught its apportioned number of fish (according to the Councils). Maryland anglers, meanwhile, have had much lower catches in recent years and thus have not found such drastic increases in the limit necessary to squelch overall harvest numbers.

CONSERVATION ORGANIZATIONS

For the future of our great sport, it's important for anglers everywhere to get involved and have their voices hear on important saltwater fisheries and conservation issues. Two outstanding non-profit organizations that do a fantastic job of representing recreational anglers are the Recreational Fishing Alliance (RFA) and the Coastal Conservation Association (CCA). Remember that in order for your voice as an angler to be heard, your support of groups like these is imperative. They have the ability to lobby politicians, send representatives to regulatory hearings and meetings, and make sure that the recreational angling community has a channel of communication to the rule-makers. Plus, by joining these organizations and going to a meeting or two you can meet other like-minded people and build a network for information-sharing when you have a hard time figuring out where the fish are biting.

To learn more about the Recreational Fishing Alliance, visit www.joinrfa.org, or call (888) 564-6732. The website for the Coastal Conservation Association is www.joincca.org. The CCA can be called at (713) 626-4234.

CHAPTER 2

KNOTS, RIGS AND TERMINAL TACKLE

Five basic knots will get you through most flounder fishing situations. A couple are easy to tie, a few others are more challenging. Master these knots and you can tie up your own rigs at your home workbench, and meet practically every need that may pop up on the water.

Every knot requires your undivided attention. Even if it's a knot you've tied 10,000 times before. Even if it's raining, windy, cold and your fingers are just about numb. Even if the fish are biting like crazy and you're desperate to get a bait back in the water. That's because even the slightest miscue when tying a knot may result in the knot slipping, or breaking, under the pressure of a hooked fish. Do not risk the heartbreak of losing the largest flounder of your lifetime to a bad knot. Take your time and concentrate, and make sure each knot is tied correctly. If there's any doubt in your mind whatsoever about a knot you've tied, then cut it off and tie it again. Get it right–knots are critically important!

The following diagrams, which show us the steps involved in tying knots, are provided by the Recreational Boating and Fishing Foundation (RBFF). The Recreational Boating and Fishing Foundation (RBFF) is a nonprofit organization established in 1998 to increase participation in recreational boating and fishing and thereby, increase public awareness and appreciation of the need for protecting, conserving and restoring the nation's aquatic natural resources. RBFF helps people discover, share and protect the legacy of boating and fishing through national outreach programs like the Take Me Fishing campaign.

Through national print, television and online advertising and its Web site, Take Me Fishing promotes recreational boating and fishing as unmatched leisure activities for true connection to family, friends and the natural world, and provides first-time anglers and boaters with "How to" and "Where to" information to get started.

There are other reasons you should know about TakeMeFishing.org, and other ways you can utilize it. TakeMeFishing.org has the Web's largest database of fishing and boating spots with 10,000 searchable locations in all 50 states. The Web site includes license, regulation, registration, safety and event information and also features "Family Friendly Hot Spots," which are places to fish and boat that offer conveniences for families such as parking, restrooms, shore access boat ramps and an abundance of fish. For more information about RBFF, visit www.RBFF.org or call (703) 519-0013. Now—on to the knots!

THE IMPROVED CLINCH

This is perhaps the most frequently used knot of them all. For most of us, when we were young, the first knot our father, grandfather, older brother or uncle taught us how to tie was the improved clinch knot. And for good reason, as it's simple and strong. For flounder fishermen, the improved clinch is a great knot for tying a three-way swivel or swivel to the end of monofilament line, or tying a hook, bucktail, or leadhead with plastic to the end of a mono or fluorocarbon leader.

A couple of quick, yet important, notes: In Step One, never make less than five, or more than seven, twists around the standing line. Less than five twists and the knot will be too weak. More than seven twists may cause the knot to jam, and weaken, as it is pulled tight.

An improved clinch knot is easy to tie with monofilament up to 30-pound test. Heavier mono and fluorocarbon can create some challenges, as it can be difficult to get the coils to draw up tightly. With heavier line, a good alternative is to tie a clinch knot, instead of an improved clinch knot. With a clinch knot, the tag end is not passed through the large loop as described in Step One. Instead, the line is tightened after five twists are made and the tag end is passed through the loop that is formed at the eye of the hook.

#1

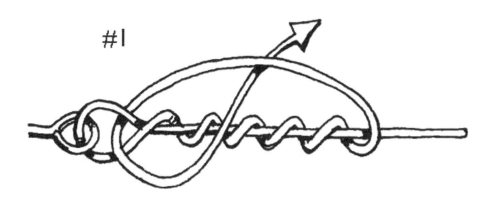

#1: Pass the line through the eye of a hook, lure or swivel. With the end of the line, make five to seven twists around the standing line. Pass the tag end through the loop formed at the eye of the hook. As the tag end is passed through the loop at the eye of the hook, a larger loop is created. After passing the tag end through the loop at the eye, pass it through the large loop.

#2

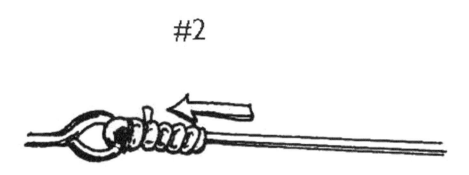

#2: While holding the standing line and the free end, pull the coils tight. Make sure the coils set up next to each other and are not crisscrossed.

THE PALOMAR

As easy and strong as an improved clinch knot is, do not tie an improved clinch in braided or "super" lines. Because those high-tech lines are very thin and usually slick, an improved clinch knot will often slip. Manufacturers of braided lines highly recommend using a palomar knot, instead, when tying on a lure, hook or swivel. A palomar is also easy to tie, stronger than an improved clinch, and it will not slip, even when jolted by savage strikes and strong hooksets. Flounder fishermen will find a palomar knot to be very useful when tying a bucktail, or a leadhead jig with a soft plastic tail, directly to the end of a braid line. A palomar can be difficult to tie when attaching a bigger plug or lure, especially if it has a treble hook. That's because the lure must be passed through a loop in the line, and a treble hook will often catch on the line and foul the knot. However, this typically isn't a problem with fluke fisherman as most of their artificals are not too big for a palomar knot, and they almost never have treble hooks.

#1: At the end of the line or leader, double it back to create a loop and pass the loop through the eye of the lure, hook or swivel.

#2: Let the lure, hook or swivel hang loose and tie an overhand knot in the double line.

#3: Pull the loop far enough to pass over the lure, hook or swivel.

#4: Pull both the tag end and standing line to tighten, and clip the tag end close to the knot.

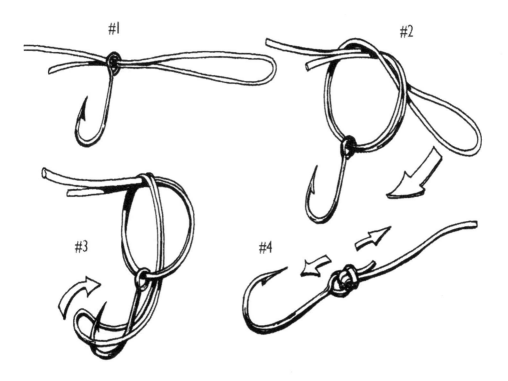

THE SURGEON'S LOOP

This knot creates a loop at the end of the line or leader. Fluke fishermen often use a surgeon's loop when creating their own bottom rigs, and a loop at the end of the line is needed to hold the sinker. Always use a rig that terminates in a loop for your sinkers, instead of tying sinkers directly to the line or leader. This will allow you to put the loop through the eye of the sinker, slide it over the bottom of the sinker then pull it tight, as opposed to knotting your line. When the wind, water depth, or tidal conditions change and a heavier or lighter sinker is needed, it's much easier to slip the loop back off the sinker and swap it out for another weight than it is to tie, cut and re-tie.

#1: Double back a few inches of line and tie it in an overhand knot, but don't pull it tight. Bring the doubled line through once again.

#2: Hold the standing line and the tag end and pull the loop to tighten the knot. Clip the tag end close to the knot.

THE DROPPER LOOP

This knot creates a loop mid-line or mid-leader. Flounder fishermen commonly use dropper loops in hand-tied top/bottom rigs to attach a hook, or a leadered hook, above the sinker. In this manner, a dropper loop is used much like a three-way swivel would be. A hook can be put on the dropper loop by slipping the loop through the eye of the hook and then over the hook itself, before being pulled tight and snugged back up against the eye. Another approach is to cut one leg of the loop near the line or leader to create a single, longer leader onto which a hook can be tied. Typing a dropper loop is a little trickier than some other knots, yet with a little practice, a dropper loop soon becomes easy to tie.

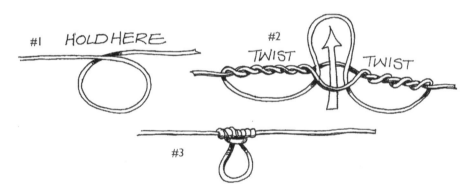

#1: Fold the line or leader back over itself to form a loop.

#2: Pull one side of the loop down and begin making turns with it around the standing line. Keep open the point where the turns are made so there are an equal number of turns on each side. After eight to 10 turns, reach through the center opening and pull the main loop through. Put your finger through this loop so it won't slip back.

#3: Hold the loop with your mouth and pull both strands of the line, tightening the coils. Release the loop and pull hard to set the knot. The tightening coils will cause the dropper to stand out from the line.

THE BLOOD KNOT

This knot is used to provide a direct connection between the mono or braided line from the reel to a mono or fluorocarbon leader (eliminating the need for a swivel). The blood knot is a low-profile knot that can be reeled through the guides and onto the reel (unlike a swivel), which may be of benefit when casting, or when bringing a hooked flounder to the net.

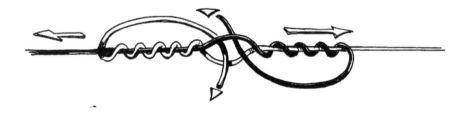

#1: Turn the end of the leader material around the end of the line five times, then tuck the tag end between the line and leader. Then, turn the end of the line five times around the leader, and tuck the tag end, in the opposite direction of the first tag end. Then steadily pull to tighten the coils, and trim both tag ends.

NOTES ON KNOTS

Most knots should be moistened before they are drawn tight to reduce friction and the heat it can cause when knots are snugged tight (a little bit of saliva will do the trick). Pull knots tight with a steady, even pressure (do not jerk them tight). Use a fingernail clipper to cut the tag end. A knife can nick the knot or leader, weakening it considerably. Never use a lighter or lit cigarette to cut with, as the heat could weaken the line or leader.

After tying, closely examine each knot to make sure it looks good. As you're fishing, occasionally check all knots, leader and line to make sure they're not nicked or chafing. If there's any sign of damage, cut and replace the knot and/or line, as necessary. Never overlook how important knots are to successful fishing!

The five knots that we've diagrammed and discussed are basic yet important knots. Eventually there are other knots you should learn as well, such as the uni-knot, spider hitch, Albright knot, surgeon's knot, and snelling a hook. But the five knots just described will provide a great foundation for your flounder fishing adventures, and will enable you to tie up the fluke rigs we're about to discuss.

TYING YOUR OWN RIGS

There are two basic requirements that any fluke rig, whether homemade or commercially produced, must meet to be effective. First, it must present live baits (minnows, spot, bluefish), whole dead baits (squid) and strip baits (squid, croaker, bluefish, sea robin) in the fluke's strike zone, which is on or very near the bottom. Yet at the same time, it should do so without dragging the bait across the bottom. Secondly, as the boat drifts or the angler retrieves line, the rig must swim, move or flutter the bait in an enticingly lifelike manner. Any rig that doesn't do both will be a dud.

In saltwater tackle shops from New England to North Carolina, the shelves feature dozens of bottom fishing rigs that will trigger strikes from fluke. They include, but are not limited to, Aqua Clear rigs, Spin 'n Glo rigs, Sea Striker rigs, and many, many others. Some anglers call them "fluke killers" and others call them "flounder pounders." A lot of tackle shops also make and sell their own specialty fluke rigs. From shallow back bays to the ocean depths, from pier fishing to trolling, there is no shortage of fluke rigs on the market.

We can take our pick of these rigs or we can separately purchase the leaders, hooks, swivels, plastic skirts, bucktail and other materials we need to create our own homemade rigs. We can customize rigs so they're ideally suited for the depths, current and type of structure we typically encounter in our favorite fluke fishing locations. And there's a special sense of personal satisfaction that comes

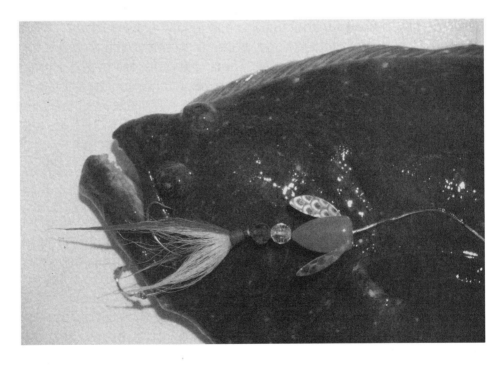

A Spin 'n Glo rig, featuring spinning blades, beads and bucktail, baited with strips of squid or cut bait, is one of the many bottom rigs that will trigger strikes from fluke.

with catching fish on rigs we tie up ourselves.

Now we're going to discuss how to use the knots that were described and diagramed earlier in this chapter to tie up productive flounder rigs. Some are pretty straightforward, featuring nothing more than a short length of leader material, a hook, and a sinker. However, you can always use your fishing knowledge and creativity, to make much more elaborate rigs that feature hardware and fish-attracting enhancements such as beads, spinnerblades, bucktail hair and plastic skirts in enough color combinations to make a peacock jealous.

FISH-FINDER AND EGG SINKER RIGS

A fish-finder is a small plastic sleeve with a clip attached (Sea Striker Duoloc Sinker Slides are one of several models you'll find in tackle shops all along the coast). When rigging up, the main line from the reel is threaded through the plastic sleeve, and then a swivel is tied to the end of the main line with an improved clinch knot or a palomar knot. About 36 inches of leader with a hook tied or snelled on the end is then tied to the other end of the swivel. The clip on the fish-finder holds the sinker. The swivel prevents the fish-finder with the sinker attached from sliding down the line to the hook. The key advantage of a fish-finder rig is that when a fluke grabs the bait and the angler "drops back" by allowing line to come freely off the reel (more on this tactic later!) the fluke can pull on the bait without dragging or detecting the weight of the sinker, as line will be pulled through the sleeve.

Fish-finder rigs work especially well when fishing live bait such as spot, snapper blues, and peanut bunker. When a fluke grabs a live bait and begins to gobble it down, the angler can give the fluke the line and time it needs to get the bait well into its mouth. Some anglers call this "feeding" the fluke, or "letting it run." Other anglers may drop the rod tip as far as possible to accomplish the same thing, allowing the fish to take the bait all the way into its mouth without ever feeling any resistance from the weight.

Once the fish has the bait well into its mouth, the drop back is complete. Then it's time to engage the reel, take up all slack until the weight of the fluke is detected on the line, and set the hook. Another benefit of the fish-finder rig is that the swivel clip on the rig means that sinkers can be changed very quickly, without cutting and re-tying.

A simple egg sinker rig works well when fishing in the surf, on piers, and in shallow-water locations. It features nothing more than a lightweight egg sinker, a small swivel, a bead and a hook. The line from the reel is threaded through the egg sinker, and then the swivel is tied to the end of the line. Tied to the other end of the swivel is a three foot leader with a hook tied on or snelled on the other end.

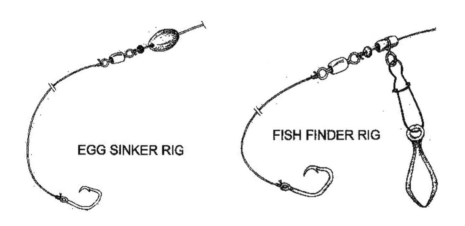

An egg sinker and fishfinder rig; use 'em with live baits.

HIGH/LOW (TOP/BOTTOM) RIG

If one bait is good, two must be even better, right? That's true in some situations, but since two hooks at different depths is a recipe for snags when fishing some kinds of structure, it's not necessarily the best pick at all times. This two-hook rig presents one bait just above the bottom, and another bait about two feet above it. To a flounder laying flat on the sand, it must appear as if a small school of bait is passing overhead, or that one baitfish is chasing another. That's often just the ticket for triggering a flounder's predatory instinct, prompting it to explode off the bottom to devour one of the baits.

To tie a top/bottom rig, create a loop at one end of a four foot, 30 pound or 40 pound test monofilament or fluorocarbon leader, by tying a surgeon's loop knot (this will be the very bottom of the rig). Then, several inches above the loop, create an in-leader loop by tying a dropper loop knot. Then, 12 to 20 inches higher in the leader, create another in-leader loop with another dropper loop knot. A swivel is tied to the top end of the leader, so it can be used to connect the rig to your main line.

Tie a fairly long bottom loop, and then cut one leg of the bottom loop near the knot, making a long single-line leader that's twice as long as the loop was before it was cut. An improved clinch knot can then be used to tie a hook onto the end of the single-line leader. Do not cut the top dropper loop. The loop is pinched down, threaded through the eye of a hook, and then the loop is opened so the hook can be passed through it, securing the hook on the loop. Keeping this top hook on a shorter, stiffer leash will prevent it from sagging down and tangling with the bottom leader or hook.

The original loop that was tied at the end (bottom) of the leader with the surgeon's loop knot is used to hold the sinker. Just like the hook on the top loop, the sinker can be changed quickly and easily, without cutting and re-tying, but buy simply doubling the loop back over the weight.

When fishing in relatively shallow water where it doesn't take too big of a sinker to hold bottom, some anglers like to replace the sinker with a bucktail tipped with a squid strip. The bucktail will provide the weight needed to keep the rig on or near the bottom, while also offering fluke yet a third bait on this rig to strike. Note, however, that some states do limit anglers to two hooks per fishing line; make sure you check the regulations for the particular area you plan to fish, before tying a rig in this fashion.

A top/bottom rig works well when drifting over shoals, sloughs and other sandy or mud bottom areas that are free of obstructions. However, they are not recommend them when fishing in and around wrecks, artificial reefs and rockpiles. Having two hooks at differing depths on the rig will only increase the number of times it gets snagged. These type of "sticky" areas are best worked with a single-hook rig.

Top/bottom rigs sold in many tackle shops feature wire holders that prevent the two leaders and hooks from tangling with each other. There's also a clip on the bottom to hold the sinker. Generations of anglers have used these rigs to catch countless numbers of fish, everything from sea bass to stripers, blowfish to bluefish, and flounder to hardhead. They work. However, I'll only use them when I'm "panfishing" for spot and croaker. When it comes to fluke fishing, I much prefer to catch fish on rigs I have created myself from mono or fluorocarbon, featuring only the hooks, swivels and other materials in the size and color I choose, whether it be bucktail hair, plastic skirts, beads, or spinnerblades.

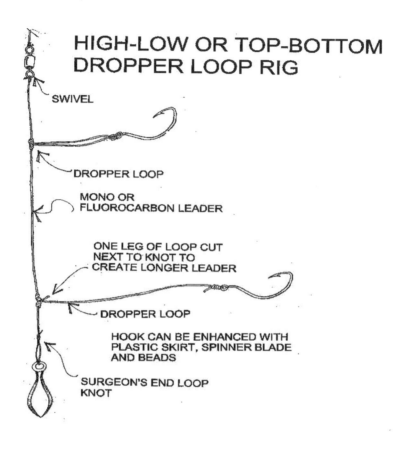

HIGH-LOW OR TOP-BOTTOM DROPPER LOOP RIG

SWIVEL

DROPPER LOOP

MONO OR
FLUOROCARBON LEADER

ONE LEG OF LOOP CUT
NEXT TO KNOT TO
CREATE LONGER LEADER

DROPPER LOOP

HOOK CAN BE ENHANCED WITH
PLASTIC SKIRT, SPINNER BLADE
AND BEADS

SURGEON'S END LOOP
KNOT

Top/bottom rigs are popular because they're so productive.

**Reaping the rewards of a good day dragging baits on top/
bottom rigs.**

THREE-WAY SWIVEL RIG

The three-way swivel rig is an alternative which allows you to fish either multiple or single baits, and has some advantages of its own. To create one, begin by tying the line from the reel to one eye of a three-way swivel. To the bottom of the swivel, tie on a six to 12 inch length of mono. At the other end of the mono, tie a surgeon's

THREE-WAY SWIVEL RIG

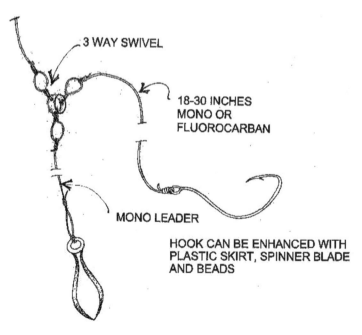

3 WAY SWIVEL

18-30 INCHES
MONO OR
FLUOROCARBAN

MONO LEADER

HOOK CAN BE ENHANCED WITH
PLASTIC SKIRT, SPINNER BLADE
AND BEADS

When losing rigs is a distinct possibility, a three-way rig is usually a better choice than the standard top/bottom rig.

end knot to form a loop which will hold the sinker (in shallow water, it is possible to replace the sinker with a bucktail, as described in the top/bottom rig). On the other swivel eye, tie a 12 to 24 inch length of 30 pound test mono or fluorocarbon leader. The hook is tied or snelled onto the other end of the leader. Strip baits and live baits can all be fished on a three-way swivel rig.

A three-way swivel rig usually snags less than a multiple-hook top/bottom rig and also works well when trolling. When the current begins to slow and then eventually quits at the end of a tide, don't just sit there in a motionless boat with an unattractive, dead-still bait soaking on the bottom. Instead, maximize your fishing time by cranking up the motor and trolling. Keeping your bait moving, even when there is no current and/or wind to push the boat, will keep your bait appealing to flatties.

Trolling is also a great way to work submerged rockpiles. As an example, Virginia anglers each year catch plenty of jumbo eight to 14 pound doormats while trolling big strip baits over the submerged boulders at the Chesapeake Bay Bridge Tunnel (the CBBT), at the mouth of Chesapeake Bay. It's a highly specialized, and very challenging way to flounder fish—yet it's also very effective. And anglers in the know fish with a slightly tweaked three-way swivel rig commonly used for flounder trolling at the CBBT, and it will catch fluke on rockpiles anywhere along the East Coast. Before looking at the rig itself, take note of the fact that rockpile trollers often spool their reels with braided or superlines, or even wire line, since they cut through the water better than mono and help keep the rig in close contact with the bottom.

Using a palomar knot, tie a three-way swivel onto the end of the line from the reel. Your hook line should have plenty of length; many trollers like leaders as long as 20 feet tied to the second eye of the swivel. One to three feet of monofilament is tied to the third eye of the swivel, and on the other end of this piece of mono, tie a surgeon's loop to create a loop that will be used to hold the sinker. Use light monofilament, say eight or ten pound test, to hold the sinker. (Sinkers of at least eight to 10 ounces are typically needed to maintain sustained contact with the bottom while trolling over the rocks in high-current areas like the CBBT rockpiles). When a rig hangs up, it's often the sinker that's snagged. If attempts to free the rig fail, then tighten down your drag to apply pressure. That light line will be the weak link, and will break away fairly easily. The sinker will be lost, but the hook and swivel above it will be saved.

This is a heavy-duty rig that works well on rocks in relatively deep water, when wind and current are also factors that need to be accounted for. For other types of trolling situations, the rig can be modified by shortening the length of the leader to the hook, shorten-

ROCK PILE TROLLING RIG

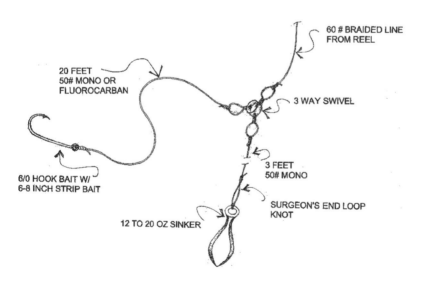

Up to 20 feet of 50 pound test monofilament or fluorocarbon leader is tied to the third eye of the swivel. A 5/0 or 6/0 hook is snelled to the other end of the leader.

ROCK PILE DRIFT RIG

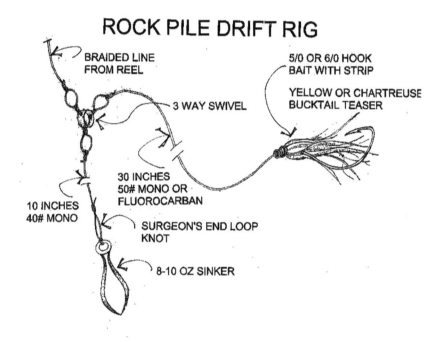

BRAIDED LINE
FROM REEL

5/0 OR 6/0 HOOK
BAIT WITH STRIP

YELLOW OR CHARTREUSE
BUCKTAIL TEASER

3 WAY SWIVEL

30 INCHES
50# MONO OR
FLUOROCARBAN

10 INCHES
40# MONO

SURGEON'S END LOOP
KNOT

8-10 OZ SINKER

Modify the rig slightly, for drift fishing.

ing the sinker leader, and using lighter sinkers.

A similar rig is used when drifting for big fluke on rockpiles, as opposed to trolling for them. In this case, the three-way swivel is again tied to the end of the braided main line with a palomar knot. To the bottom eye of the swivel, tie on about a foot of monofilament, with a loop tied in the other end to hold the sinker. On the final eye of the three-way swivel, a clinch knot is used tie on a two-foot piece of 50-pound test fluorocarbon leader. You may want to add some color and additional attraction in the form of yellow or chartreuse hair teasers, or plastic squid bodies, which are slipped on the leader just ahead of the hook. Bait up with a long strip bait.

The clear and informative diagrams that illustrate the rigs were provided by Capt. Bruce Kaufman. My brother has caught his share of flounder in Delaware and Chesapeake Bays, even though most of his fishing now is for tuna, marlin, dolphin and wahoo on the offshore grounds. Thanks, Bruce, for the diagrams!

TERMINAL TACKLE

When a flounder opens up to eat, its mouth is wide and gaping. And, a wide variety of hooks in sizes 2/0 to 4/0, will catch that flounder.

English-style wide-bend hooks, or Kahle hooks, have caught lots of flounder over the years. They're often the hook of choice among anglers who tie their own top/bottom rigs, and they're commonly found on commercial fluke rigs because they are especially effective when fishing strips of squid, croaker, spot and bluefish, or the popular squid-minnow sandwich. (Mustad and Owner are two of the many companies that market Kahle hooks.)

Another popular hook for strip baits is the Pacific Bass hook; a key advantage of this hook is its long shank, which is easier to unhook from a flounder because the shank can be grabbed with fingers or pliers and worked free from the fish.

Octopus-style hooks (Gamakatsu, VMC and others) also get a lot of play from fluke fishing enthusiasts.

When targeting doormat flounder with live baits such as spot and snapper bluefish, many fluke experts rely on thin wire bait hooks such as the Owner Mutu Light. The thin wire won't kill a live bait as quickly as a regular hook, and the less-restrictive light wire enables it to swim and move about more freely and more naturally.

Short-shank live bait hooks also do an excellent job of offering up spot, bluefish and other live baits to big fluke.

Circle hooks and colored hooks, have come on strong in the fluke fishing game in recent years. Nearly all major hook companies, including Eagle Claw, Spro, Gamakatsu, Owner, VMC and others, offer circle hooks. Because of the bend very near the point of circle hooks, I find it a bit more difficult to put a bait on them, particularly a squirming live bait. However, it's well worth it, as each year non-offset circle hooks save many undersized flounder from an unnecessary death. That's because a circle hook almost always catches a flounder, or any fish for that matter, at the corner of the mouth. Non-offset circle hooks do not gut-hook fish, as standard J hooks can. Circle hooks in the corner of a fish's mouth also makes it much easier to unhook and release fish with minimal handling and less damage to the fish, especially important when releasing undersized fluke that don't measure up to the minimum size limit.

Remember that offset circle hooks—those which have a point and shank that are not on a parallel plane—do not always have the same effect as non-offset circle hooks. Many offset circle hooks regularly do hook fish in the gut, doing just as much damage as a J hook. Most of the time the packages of hooks are well marked, but if you're not sure if your circle hooks are offset or non-offset, simply lay one down on a table. If the point curves up off of the table, it's offset. If it lies flat on a parallel plane with the shank of the hook, it's non-offset.

Do not jerk back your rod to set the hook in a fish's mouth when fishing with a circle hook. Instead, when a fluke has picked up the bait just pause for a couple of seconds and then begin reeling. This will move the circle hook to the corner of the mouth where it will dig in and hook the fluke.

Fluke fishermen, and many other anglers for that matter, have been seeing red in recent years. That's because colored hooks, especially red, have been hot items. The theory is that red hooks add to the appearance of a bleeding, injured baitfish, or that the flash of red from the hooks resembles a fish's flaring gills, both of which trigger strikes from predators such as fluke. English-style wide-gap hooks, Pacific bass hooks, octopus hooks, live bait hooks and circle hooks

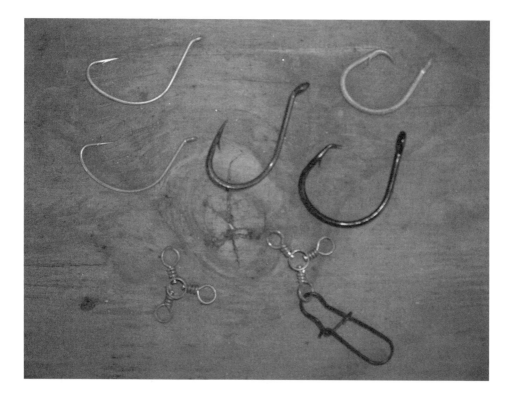

Wide-bend hooks, bait hooks, circle hooks and three-way swivels commonly used on many flounder rigs.

are all available in red.

It used to be that anglers sharpened their hooks right out of the box, but today, high-tech chemical and laser hook sharpening processes are used by many hook manufacturers. These result in hooks that are super sharp right out of the box. There is no need to touch them up with a file. In fact, many of today's hooks are so well sharpened that anything we do to them will actually dull them. Use them as they come, check the point occasionally, and when a hook seems to have dulled, tie on a new one.

Swivels are another important piece of terminal tackle. Don't skimp on them—buy good ones, ball-bearing swivels with either solid rings or split rings, to connect the rig to the end of the line from the reel, because ball-bearing swivels will reduce and even eliminate line twist. If you often get tangles in your line from too much twist, cheap swivels are probably the culprit.

Many anglers prefer non-reflective black swivels, as the flash of brass or stainless steel swivels will often attract the attention of hungry, toothy bluefish. A bluefish biting the swivel can easily cut the line or leader, resulting in lost tackle. Or, even worse, a bite from a bluefish may nick the line or leader, which will probably give way when a doormat fluke is hooked.

Sinkers are also, of course, necessary tackle for flounder fishing. Use enough weight to keep a fluke rig on or near the bottom. A sinker that's too light will rise up off the bottom, lifting the rig out of the flounder strike zone. In a shallow back bay a one-half ounce sliding egg sinker may be perfect, while out in the ocean it may require eight, 10, even 20 ounces to effectively hold bottom.

When fishing in and around rockpiles, wrecks and artificial reefs, in-line sinkers, typically used in trolling for striped bass and other species, are recommended over dipsy, or "bank" style sinkers. Their advantage is their narrow-profile, which will cut down on the number of snags that would have occurred with a wider-profile or bulkier sinker; these skinnier sinkers simply slide in and out of tight spots that would have snagged a wider sinker.

TEASERS

Bucktail hair tied on a small sleeve can be threaded on the leader to provide an additional attractant, commonly called a "teaser." Fluke fishermen usually favor white bucktail, or bucktail that's been dyed green, chartreuse, yellow or pink.

Plastic squid skirts or squid bodies are also popular teasers among flounder pounders. They're threaded on the leader so the tentacles hang back over the hook and bait, and flutter as the rig moves through the water. Squid skirts that are two and a half to seven inches long are commonly used on fluke rigs. Boone squid skirts,

**Plastic squid skirts are often used to provide
extra attraction to a bottom rig.**

Tsunami Squids, Salmon Squid Bodies and Pline Bulb Squids are among the varieties that are available in most tackle shops.

Beads are another form of eye-catching teaser. Along with extra color, they also provide a rig with some protection from abrasion. It's a good idea to thread one or more beads on the line between a fish-finder rig and the swivel, or between an egg sinker and the swivel, as the beads will prevent the fish-finder or sinker from sliding into the knot and possibly weakening it.

Spinner blades are also used as teasers when flounder fishing. The blades add flash and vibration, both of which help to attract fish. If a spinner blade is put on a rig via a clevis, put one or two beads on the leader both in front of and behind the clevis, which will help protect it and keep the blade spinning freely. When tying rigs with a bucktail sleeve or plastic squid skirt, anglers will often slip a couple of beads on the leader right behind the hair or plastic, so the beads provide a little separation between the bucktail or squid, and the hook.

LINE AND LEADER

Monofilament line. Braided line. Fluorocarbon leader. For the most part, these are what flounder fishermen need to spool onto their reels, and to tie up fluke-busting rigs. Some anglers choose monofilament when it comes to fishing strip baits and live baits for flounder. Unlike no-stretch, super-sensitive braided line, monofilament line will stretch, and the "cushion" that stretching provides is important when drifting baits along the bottom. Remember that when a fluke grabs a bait, the angler needs to drop back his offering before setting the hook, so the fluke can move the bait farther into its mouth without detecting resistance from the sinker or the angler. With the incredible sensitivity of braided lines, some anglers believe it's difficult to drop-back quickly enough after a pick-up to avoid having the fluke detect resistance and drop the bait. However, with mono, the stretching and the lesser sensitivity will provide an extra moment for the angler to drop back before the weight of the sinker or pull of the line will prompt the fluke to spit out the bait.

My personal favorite monofilament for flounder drifting is 14 pound or 17 pound test Sufix Siege. One of the first things you'll notice is that Siege mono comes on an extra-wide spool. The wide spool is used so the line can be put on the spool in such a way that memory is eliminated, and so the line will come off the spool and onto a reel very smoothly, for tangle-free casting. It's called Advanced G2 Precision Winding.

Many flounder anglers spool up with 12 to 20 pound test monofilament or braided line, while rigs are tied up with 30 or 40 pound test mono or fluorocarbon leader material.

Patented XV2 Technology has enabled Sufix to build into Siege line the combination all anglers are looking for: a thin-diameter line that handles well, yet still possesses the hook-setting and fish-fighting power needed to conquer barn door-size fluke and all of our favorite species. Siege is very abrasion resistant, enabling anglers to dunk baits in and among rockpiles, wrecks, bridge pilings, and other tough neighborhoods where big fluke often hang out.

Of course, there are other high-quality, high-tech monofila-ment lines that also perform very well for fluke fishermen, such as Stren, and Berkley Big-Game Trilene, just to name a couple.

Now, let's take a look at braided lines, such as Power Pro, Western Filament Tuf line, Stren Super Braid, Performance Braid by Sufix, Berkley Fire Line, Spider Wire, Power Pro, PLine Spectrex IV, Cabella's Ripcord, and Bass Pro Shops Excel Nitro line. Despite the information in the previous paragraphs, there are legions of anglers who still prefer to use braided line when drifting bait rigs for fluke.

Braided lines are also an excellent choice when bucktailing for fluke, when jigging with metal lures, and with leadheads dressed with soft plastic bodies (Bass Assassins and others). These incred-ibly strong lines feature a thinner diameter than mono of comparable strength, which means there's less water resistance on the line, en-abling the line to better keep bait rigs and artificial lures on or near the bottom. The lack of stretch of braided lines provides a very sig-nificant increase in sensitivity. You'll feel every thump when the lure hits bottom, and you'll know right away when you've lost contact with the bottom and more line needs to be played out to get the lure back in the flounder's strike zone. When a fluke does grab the bucktail or jig, you'll instantly detect the extra weight.

MARKER BUOYS

It gets real exciting when a fluke is hooked and the battle is on. As the angler fights the fish, others scramble for the net and, if necessary, they clear lines and stow items in the boat out of the way, all in the hopes of ensuring a successful catch. When the fish is netted and brought aboard it has to be unhooked, measured if necessary, and deposited in the cooler if it's big enough. As all of this is going on, the boat continues to drift, moving away from where the fluke was originally hooked.

Fluke are not spread out evenly all over the bottom, but instead usually are bunched up tight in certain spots. It can be com-

Where there's one, there are usually several. When a nice flounder is hooked, immediately enter the location in a GPS or mark it with a buoy so you can return to that exact hot spot and catch more flounder.

pared to flying over an NFL game in a blimp or a helicopter. If the ball is on the 20 yard line, you'll see most of the players (offensive and defensive linemen) positioned along both sides of the 20 yard line. The running backs and linebackers will be only a couple of yards off the 20 yard line, while three or four defensive backs will be farthest away, yet even they will only be 10 to 15 yards off the 20. Most of the field is empty. Just as football players are not evenly distributed over the field, fluke will not be all over the entire structure, instead, a majority of them will be located in close proximity to each other in a particular hot spot (productive fluke structure is described in detail in chapter six).

Flounder expert Andy Orr is always on the lookout for a "nest" of big flounder. He believes flounder of the same size school together, so when a big one is hooked, he wants to return to that exact same location so it can be fished thoroughly in hopes of catching more big flounder. No need continuing to drift or troll when you're aware of a particular spot that very well may hold more big fish. So, it's very important to mark the spot where a big fish is hooked. Someone on the boat needs to be in charge of immediately entering the location in the GPS, or another excellent way to quickly and easily mark a hot spot is with a homemade marker buoy.

An empty detergent bottle makes a great buoy. Use orange and yellow bottles that can be easily seen on the water, even at great distances. Do not use green, blue or white bottles, as they're difficult to spot. Rinse out the bottle, and screw the lid securely back on. Tie one end of a light rope, or 100 pound test mono, to the handle on the bottle. Then wrap the rope or heavy line around the bottle. At the other end of the rope or line, tie on several heavy sinkers.

Wrap the line around the bottle, so that when a fluke is hooked, all that needs to be done to mark that spot is to drop the bottle over the side of the boat. As the sinkers fall toward the bottom, they'll pull line from the bottle, which will spin on the surface. When the bottle stops spinning, the sinkers are on the bottom. The bottle floating on the surface makes it easy to return to the spot so it can be thoroughly fished. Once you're finished, swing by and pick up the bottle, and pull in the rope or line and sinkers.

I'd recommend making two or more marker buoys, each with different lengths of line. Use a permanent marker pen to write the line length on the bottle. For shallow-water fishing spots, make a marker buoy that has about 25 feet of line on it. For mid-depth locations, a buoy with 50 feet of line should work well. For deep-water summer-time fishing hot spots in the ocean, make a buoy that features 85 or even 100 feet of line.

Maintaining an updated log book will make you a more knowledgeable fisherman and will enable you to hook into more flounder, more often.

LOG BOOK

A log book is a valuable, yet often overlooked, fishing tool. After every trip, whether fish were caught or not, jot down the details in a log book. Important details include the date and time of the fishing trip, the specific locations fished, the water depths and the structure that were fished, the rigs and baits and lures that were used at each spot, the tidal and current conditions, the phase of the moon, weather conditions including wind speed and direction, who you fished with, and the most productive rigs (including colors), baits and lures at each location.

I strongly recommend that you write all of this data down no later than the very next morning after the trip, while all of the details are still fresh in your mind. The more fishing trips that are entered into a log book, the more valuable it becomes, as certain patterns will become evident. During the winter, when there's no flounder fishing, spend a considerable amount of time reviewing your log books, and use the information they contain to begin planning fluke fishing trips for the upcoming season.

CHAPTER 3

RODS, REELS, AND USING THEM EFFECTIVELY

The most important thing to keep in mind when choosing rods ands reels is that you should use tackle that is comfortable, and works for you. Familiarity with your tackle builds confidence, and confidence will make you a more successful fluke fisherman. Occasionally try different types of tackle to determine what best suits your needs for different fluke fishing situations.

SPINNING VS. BAITCASTING VS. CONVENTIONAL REELS

Spinning reels on six and a half to seven foot rods are typically used when it's necessary to cast and retrieve rigs or lures. Anglers fishing from the beach, piers, jetties, bridges and sometimes boats, usually cast for flounder with spinning reels as they're easy to use and provide good casting accuracy. The major down-side to spinning reels is that they tend to place twist into your line during retrieval.

When drifting in a boat for flounder, rigs and lures are typically dropped straight down to the bottom for drifting or trolling. Many flounder anglers prefer baitcasting reels or small conventional reels on six foot rods for this type of fishing. They are easy to use and provide good line control when drifting. However, remember that it's a matter of personal preference, and there are plenty of anglers who drift fish with spinning reels. And, there is a down-side to baitcasting reels, too: they take significantly more finesse to use and even the experts will experience bird's nests now and again.

Conventional reels are a good choice when trolling for flounder. Sturdy conventional reels on rods of six and a half to eight feet in length provide the muscle and control needed to troll with heavy sinkers in deeper water which will overpower most lighter gear. These reels are tough if not impossible to cast, however, and their heavy nature may squelch the fight of smaller fish.

Before purchasing a reel, check the drag to make sure it

**Spinning reels are most commonly used when drifting bottom rigs,
and when casting from bridges, jetties and in the surf.**

doesn't jump or stick, and that it yields line smoothly. On spinning reels, take a close look at the guide on the bail to make sure it turns smoothly. Baitcasting or conventional reels commonly used for flounder fishing feature levelwinds. If not, the angler must use his thumb to evenly distribute line on the reel as line is reeled in, or the line will pile up in one spot and create a tangle.

While rods and reels can seem somewhat expensive, with proper care and maintenance, they will provide years of reliable service. Quality tackle is made by companies including Shimano, Daiwa, Quantum, Okuma, Abu Garcia, Fenwick, Penn, Cabella's, Bass Pro Shops and others. Generally speaking, the more ball bearings in a reel, the smoother and more dependable its performance will be. Inexpensive rods and reels may save a few bucks in the short term, but they may create headaches in the form of poor performance, and may eventually cost more in repairs.

RODS

Graphite rods are everywhere, and for good reason: they're lightweight, strong and sensitive. Some rods feature graphite reel seats for even more sensitivity, so you can better detect when a fluke has subtly picked up a bait. Anglers have their choice of EVA foam, or cork, rod grips and butts. Ceramic and oxide guides reduce line wear and dissipate heat caused by friction from the line moving over the guides, especially under pressure of a heavy fish. Be sure the weight of the sinkers or lures to be used matches the rod, and the lines that are used.

Rod action also needs to be considered. Generally, it's best to avoid rods that have a lot of flex or sweep in the tip (slow-action rods). The flex makes them less effective when it comes to jigging with bucktails, leadheads or metal lures, and also when bouncing bait rigs along the bottom. On the other hand, fast-action rods provide more control over bait rigs and lures, and also quicker, more powerful hooksets.

Special, heavy-duty tackle is needed when drifting or trolling for doormat flounder on rockpiles. Large conventional reels with levelwinds, spooled with 20 pound mono or 30 pound braided line, and matched with sturdy, stiff rods are needed for the eight to ten ounce sinkers that are used when drifting the rocks. Trollers spool up with braided line or braided wire line and send their rigs to the rocks with 12 to 20 ounce sinkers. Drifting and trolling rockpiles are challenging and specialized ways to fish for flounder, and they require the heaviest tackle you'll need for flounder fishing.

When fishing with live bait, and also bottom rigs dressed with strip baits, developing a feel for the drop-back we talked about earlier is a very important aspect of fluke fishing. When fishing for fluke, you must constantly remind yourself that it's important NOT to set the hook when a fluke first grabs the bait. An immediate hookset usually pulls the bait away from the fish without it getting hooked. Dropping back involves pausing when a strike is detected, and many anglers (but not all) provide line so the fluke can continue to eat the bait without the bait being pulled away from it, and without the fluke detecting resistance from the sinker and/or angler.

GEAR CHOICES AND THE DROP-BACK

How does the drop-back relate to rods and reels? Many fluke experts will tell you that it's easier to drop-back with baitcasting reels than with spinning reels, since the mission can be completed with the press of a button. There are, however, several ways line can be provided to the fluke when it first strikes.

Here's a common approach to the drop-back with baitcasting gear: To control the line on the reel, you'll let your offering down to the bottom by pressing down on the spool of your baitcasting reel with your thumb, then pushing the button or flipping the lever, to disengage the spool. Then relax the pressure being applied with your thumb, until the weight of the sinker pulls line off the reel and the rig sinks toward the bottom. Soon, you will feel the "thump" of the sinker striking the bottom, which tells you the rig is now in the fluke strike zone. When the thump is detected, press down your thumb on the spool once again. Do not, however, flip the lever or push the button. Instead, you want the spool to remain disengaged while line is no longer coming off of the reel, because you have stopped the spool with your thumb.

As the boat drifts along, you should feel your sinker occasionally striking the bottom. If contact with bottom if lost, momentarily lift your thumb so additional line can come off the reel, enabling the rig to sink back to the bottom, then press down again with your thumb. This process can be repeated once or twice until the rig gets too far

Baitcasting and small conventional reels are commonly used while drifting for flounder. Many anglers leave the reel disengaged and control the spool and line with their thumb.

from the boat for effective fishing. (Then it's time to reel up, check the bait, put on fresh bait, if necessary, and start over.)

When a fluke takes that bait, it may whack it with gusto or pick it up subtly. Whether it's a jolting strike or you simply detect extra weight on the end of the line, you should immediately lift your thumb so line can come off with the spool with no resistance—now, you're dropping back the bait. Over the next few moments the flounder will clamp down to injure its prey, then move it farther back into its mouth. If you set the hook the moment you feel that bite, you'll probably come up empty. Or, if the fluke detects the weight of the sinker or meets with resistance from an angler who does not give line, it may spit the bait. Dropping back for several seconds will give the fish the few moments it needs to continue eating the bait and get that hook right where you need it to be.

What if you prefer spinning gear to baitcasting gear? Some anglers who use spinning reels will leave the bail open and will hold and control the line with their index finger. When a strike or pickup is detected, they will immediately straighten their finger to drop the line. This enables line to come freely off the spool, so the fluke does not detect resistance and so the bait is not pulled away from the fish, providing it with a few moments to get the bait, and the hook, farther into its mouth.

HOW TO DO IT HEAVY

There are other ways of dropping back and hooking flounder that do not involve allowing line to come off the reel. Andy Orr is a flounder fishing expert who, along with his father and friends, uses unique and productive tactics to catch lots of big flounder in Delaware Bay each year, in the 25 to 32 foot depths at the Cross Ledge and near the Flat Top lighthouse out of Money Island, New Jersey. Andy uses heavier sinkers than many flounder fishermen. Where four or six ounces would be enough to hold bottom, Andy typically uses eight, 10 or even 12 ounce sinkers. There are times when he'll even bulk up with hefty 18 and 20 ounce sinkers, and he does his flounder fishing with the rods in rod holders.

The heavy sinkers keep Andy's rigs on or near the bottom, without the need to occasionally let out more line. The hefty sinkers also enable Andy to fish his rigs practically straight down, where he feels they move through the water with optimum performance. Andy says the more line that is let out, and the farther behind the boat rigs are fished, the greater the likelihood that the rigs will spin or move unnaturally through the water.

Fishing in the front of the boat, Andy usually uses three rods at a time (or as many as are legally allowed). Once Andy drops his rigs to the bottom, he engages the reels and places the rods in a rod holder. He stands watch, keeping a close eye on the rods as the sinkers bounce along the bottom (hopefully in unison). The rods bend as the drifting boat lifts the sinkers up and off the bottom. The rods straighten when the sinkers hit bottom again. This continues until a rod does something different; when a rod does not bend or straighten along with the other rods. This means a fluke has probably grabbed the bait!

Andy immediately pulls that rod out of the rod holder, and walks toward the back of the boat while lowering the rod tip. The combined motion provides a little tension-free line to the attacking fish, for the drop-back. When the motion of the boat causes the line to come tight again and the weight of the fluke is detected, Andy sets the hook hard and begins battling the hooked fluke. So while most anglers will work on giving line to the fish, Andy's quick drop-back involves only moving with the rod; he does not pay any line off of the reel. (More of Orr's interesting ideas and flounder-catching tactics are included in chapter eight.)

If after dropping back you set the hook and miss the fish, quickly disengage the spool or quickly lower the rod tip, to give line so the rig and bait can sink back to the fish. At times, determined flounder will take another whack at it, giving you a second chance to hook them.

Every day is different when it comes to fluke fishing. Some days, fluke can be very aggressive and catching them requires only a very brief drop-back. Other days they can eat a bait rather lethargically, making it necessary to drop-back several moments longer than usual. Which way works best on any given day at any given time, you'll have to work out when you're on the water.

CHAPTER 4

THE BEST BAITS

Flounder are aggressive predators. They feed by sight and by ambush, lying flat and camouflaged on the bottom while waiting for an unsuspecting meal to swim by. Then fluke explode off the bottom to attack and devour. There is an incredibly long list of fish and shellfish on the fluke menu, including (but not limited to) minnows, silversides, bunker (menhaden), eels, shrimp, worms, blue crabs, sand dollars, spot, and small bluefish, seatrout, white perch and winter flounder.

When a flounder opens wide to eat, its large mouth displays very menacing teeth. It only takes one look at a big flounder's huge, toothy mouth to realize that these fish are very capable of super-sizing their meals. Fluttering strip baits that are six, eight, even 10 inches long will be attacked by hungry fluke. Big fluke also have a hankering for big, juicy live baits. The old "big baits for big fish" saying is especially true when it comes to catching doormat fluke.

SQUID (AND SQUID SUBSTITUTES)

Squid strips are used by fishermen everywhere to catch practically everything that swims on the inshore grounds, and they are a very popular and productive fluke bait. Fished alone, a long squid strip provides a seductive fluttering action that flounder find irresistible. However, most flounder pounders choose to further enhance their squid strip with a live minnow. The squid-minnow combo is unquestionably one of the most widely-used fluke baits around, and with good reason, as it catches tons of these fish each season. The white squid strip provides eye-catching flutter that triggers an impulse to grab the bait, while the minnow provides a mouthful of meaty taste that makes the fluke want to swallow the entire affair. It's a deadly combination!

Look over squid carefully when buying it in a bait and tackle shop. You want the biggest and whitest squid you can find, so it can be sliced into long strips that will provide a tantalizing flutter when drifted on a bottom rig. Do not buy squid if it appears small, yellow or inferior in any way. If it's all you can get, use it to catch croaker, spot, perch and other fish which you can then cut into strip baits for fluke. To prepare squid for fluke fishing, pull the head and tentacles off the squid and save them as they, too, make productive baits. Then run the point of your knife into the open end of the squid body. Cut open

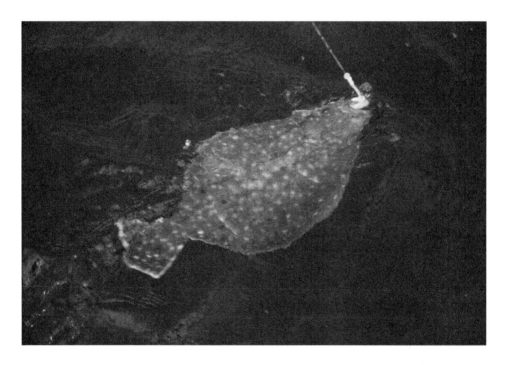

A nice flounder hooked on a squid strip.

the squid body and lay it flat. The reddish membrane on the outside of the squid should be scraped away with the knife blade. Then cut the squid into long, narrow strips that are slightly wider at one end and taper down to a point. Don't make the wide end too wide, or the strip may spin instead of fluttering through the water. Hook the strip only once through the wide end.

Squid head and tentacles should be fished on some sort of rig that features dual or tandem (two hooks tied several inches apart) hooks, as they'll prevent the bait from balling up and spinning as the rig moves through the water.

Time on the water is precious, so use as much of it as you can for fishing. This means when possible, bait cutting and preparation should be done prior to the fishing trip, usually at home the night before. Slice the squid into strips, place them in plastic bags or plastic containers, pour in some kosher salt, and store them in the freezer. There are some alternatives that are quick, easy, will keep your hands cleaner than preparing your own squid, and most importantly—they'll catch fish. For one, you can purchase colored, scented, pre-cut squid strips. Colors include white, pink, green, yellow and red, while scents include peeler crab, bunker, shrimp and bloodworm. Not only does the added scent help trigger additional strikes, it also covers human scent. Examples of commercially-prepared squid strips are Fisherman's Choice Natural Hand-Cut Bait Squid Strips (www.fisher manschoice.com), and Pro Cut Bait Squid Strips (www.procutbaits. com).

Another choice is Fishbites, which have generated an incredible amount of attention in recent years—and for good reason, as they catch fish, including fluke. Touted as "the synthetic alternative to natural cut bait," Fishbites are sold in bags and one of the Fishbites baits is its Saltwater E-Z Squid. Bloodworm is another Fishbites bait that will catch flounder. The Fishbites website is www.fishbites.com. Berkley Gulp! baits also work very well on fluke and our other favorite saltwater predators. The Berkley Gulp! Squid is not strip baits, instead, it's a six inch dead ringer for a live squid with mantle, tentacles and the whole works. Not only does it look and feel like a real squid, it also features Berkley's famous rapid scent dispersion that makes it smell like a real live squid. The scent dispersion attracts fish, triggers them to strike, and causes them to hang on to the bait longer. Other baits of interest to fluke fishermen include the Berkley Gulp! Bloodworm, and Continuous Cut Bait. Check them out on the web at www.berkley-fishing.com. All of these alternative squid baits are ready to use right out of the container, they do not need refrigeration, and they don't stink.

Pre-cut scented squid strips catch lots of fluke each season.

MINNOW

Also known as killies or mummichogs, depending on where you're from and where you fish, minnow are one of a flounder's favorite meals. While a minnow can be fished alone, many anglers use them along with a strip of squid. The classic squid-and-minnow "sandwich" has been used by generations of anglers to catch millions of fluke. The squid strip goes on the hook first, followed by the minnow, hooked through both lips.

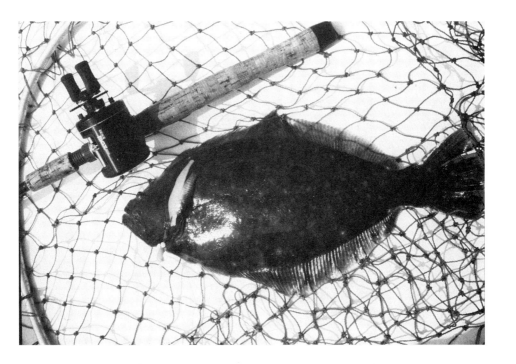

Yet another fluke that could not resist the deadly squid-minnow combination.

Minnow can be purchased at bait and tackle shops, or anglers can net, trap or catch their own. They're often kept in a baitwell, or in a bait bucket hung over the side of the boat. It seems the older I get, the more often I forget to lift the bait bucket back into the boat before I take off to re-position the boat for another drift. The bait bucket bouncing along the surface of the water creates quite a commotion; it's possible to lose the bait bucket, and the minnow in it, if the bucket's handle is broken off. That's why I prefer to keep minnows inside the boat, either in a baitwell, or even better yet, in a small cooler that does not even require water to keep them alive.

Fluke love to munch on minnows.

In preparing the cooler to hold minnows, the first thing that goes in is ice. It's best to put the ice in a sealed plastic bag so the water will be contained as the ice melts. Lay the bag of ice flat on the bottom of the cooler. If no bag is used, it will be necessary to occasionally pour off water as the ice melts. A wet towel or rag, or some wet newspaper, is then spread on top of the ice. The minnow then go on top of the wet rag or newspaper. Keep the lid on the cooler, and the coolness from the ice plus the moisture from the rag or newspaper will keep the minnows alive all day. With this type of bait cooler, you simply reach in and pluck out the minnow you want; there's no need to dip them with a small net as is required when minnows are kept in water in a baitwell.

BLUEFISH

Fresh bluefish is a very effective flounder bait. If I happen to catch a small bluefish, it is immediately placed on the bait board and prepared for use as bait. I fillet each side of the fish. From each fillet, I will slice two or three long strips; big flounder have no problem attacking strip baits up to 12 inches long. Strips should be cut so they are slightly wider at one end, narrowing down so that the other end almost comes to a point.

SEA ROBIN

Bluefish is one of my very favorite flounder baits, and fresh cut sea robin is another top choice. Strips from the upper back portion of a sea robin, where the skin and scales are dark, are just as effective as white belly strips. Sea robin skin is tough and stands up well to abuse from small hardhead and other would-be bait stealers.

SHARK

Smooth dogfish, often referred to as sand sharks, are a common catch on fluke fishing trips. They also provide durable, effective strip baits. Their tough skin makes it very, very difficult for fluke to pull the bait entirely off the hook. Unhooking a used shark strip can also be quite challenging, as getting the hook barb to come back through the skin is difficult. It's often necessary to cut the strip off the hook with a knife.

From top to bottom, sea robin, lizardfish and smooth dogfish make meaty, tough and tantalizing fluke baits.

LIVE BAITS—BLUES, BUNKER, HARDHEAD, SPOT AND PERCH

When you're fishing specifically for doormat flounder of five pounds and up, probably the best bait you can use is a small, live bluefish. Some of the largest flounder ever caught, including the IGFA All-Tackle World Record, were taken on live snapper bluefish. Bluefish and other live baits can be fished effectively using a fish-finder rig, or a sliding egg sinker rig. When drifting or trolling hook the bait through the lips, through the nostrils, or through the eye sockets. You may also want to consider hooking the bait through the back under the dorsal fin, but save this tactic for when the boat is at anchor or you're fishing from the shoreline. Otherwise, baits hooked in this fashion often spin when pulled backwards through the water by your moving boat.

With live baits, it may be a good idea to tie the hook onto the leader with a palomar knot, leaving a long tag end. A small treble hook can then be tied to the tag end, and one point of the treble hook can be hooked through the bait's tail. This "stinger" rig, as it's commonly called, provides a hook at both ends of the bait, increasing the chances a flounder will be hooked when it grabs and begins to swallow the your offering.

Many smaller flounder won't bother with these live baits, so you probably won't catch as many flounder as you would with strip baits. Your chances of catching a true doormat flounder, however, increase considerably when you're using a live offering.

Spot, croaker, herring and small white perch also make tantalizing flounder baits when live-lined near the bottom. It's usually a good idea to fish most live baits during tidal periods when the current isn't too strong; a strong current will often cause live baits to spin, regardless of how they're rigged but especially when hooked through the back.

It's important to be aware of the regulations in the state in which you are fishing. If there is a minimum size limit on bluefish, croaker or any other species that you may use for bait, then the fish used for bait must meet that minimum size requirement.

LIVE BAIT RIG

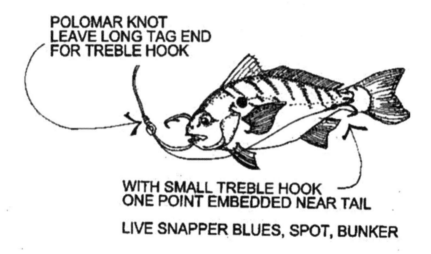

POLOMAR KNOT
LEAVE LONG TAG END
FOR TREBLE HOOK

WITH SMALL TREBLE HOOK
ONE POINT EMBEDDED NEAR TAIL

LIVE SNAPPER BLUES, SPOT, BUNKER

Live baits rigged with a stinger hook boost your chances for a hook-up.

BUNKER AND PEANUT BUNKER

Practically every predator on the inshore grounds, and in our bays and tidal rivers, loves to eat bunker. Bunker, also known as mossbunker, menhaden, pogy and fatbacks, are an incredibly important forage fish. Small bunker under six inches in length are commonly called "peanut bunker" or simply "peanuts". Unfortunately, in some areas, especially Chesapeake Bay, they've been overexploited. The resulting shortage of bunker is causing serious problems among the predators that rely on them. The problems include undersized, malnourished, and diseased fish, especially striped bass. This is an urgent situation that must be addressed, and soon, by fisheries managers!

Fortunately, there is one group dedicated to solving the situation: Menhaden Matter. This cooperative organization, made up of conservation and recreational groups (including the Chesapeake Bay Foundation, the Coastal Conservation Organization, and the Environmental Defense and National Coalition for Marine Conservation), is attempting to get current regulations changed to meet the menhaden's needs. They recommend harvest limits, shorter harvest seasons, area closures, regional quotas, and other management tools be implemented to solve the menhaden's problems. To contact Menhaden Matter and give the group your support, go to www.menhadenmatter.org.

Juvenile menhaden—peanut bunker—show up in bays and tidal rivers in the late summer and early fall. As the season progresses they migrate from creeks and coves into tributary rivers, and finally into bays. They can be hooked on Sabiki rigs, and caught in cast nets. However, they're fragile and difficult to keep alive; they won't last but a few minutes in a bucket of saltwater. The baitwell on your boat may have sufficient water flow and space to work with menhaden, or it may not. Special bait stations that keep water well aerated and constantly circulating are available in bait and tackle shops and fishing catalogs, and most do a good job of keeping bunker alive and frisky. They'll keep kicking longer if hooked through one eye socket (just in front of the eyeball) and out through the other eye socket, as opposed to hooking them through the jaws.

Schools of adult bunker can often be seen splashing and flashing on the surface of the water. The tightly-packed fish can be snagged by tossing a large weighted treble hook, or a big jighead or bucktail, into the bunker school and jerking it through the fish. Whatever is used to snag bunker, it should feature a large (8/0) hook with a wide gap. Too often, bunker snagged on hooks without a wide gap will fall off, especially as they are being lifted from the water into the boat.

A cast net may also be used to capture live bunker. In the pre-dawn hours they may be found gathered in schools below dock and bridge lights, in relatively shallow water. Once daybreak hits you can cast the net when you see menhaden flip close by, but this is a hit-or-miss proposition. When bunker move deeper than 10 feet, it becomes extremely difficult to catch them in a cast net, and a very large net is required. In shallower water a six foot net will do the job, but in water over 10 feet deep, an eight or 10 foot cast net becomes necessary, and these large nets are very difficult to throw effectively. Once you do have live bunker onboard, however, the work seems worthwhile—on the hook, flounder will go crazy for them.

LIZARDFISH

I have caught lizardfish in both Chesapeake and Delaware bays while drifting with cut bait intended for flounder, hardhead and seatrout. I have even seen these long, skinny, toothy critters caught on spoons trolled for rockfish and Spanish mackerel. Lizardfish that are six to 12 inches long make great flounder baits, either fished live on a fish-finder rig or cut into strips and fished on a typical flounder bottom rig. So, while people do not commonly target them for collection as a bait, when you do encounter a lizard fish think twice before tossing it back over the side. It may not be the number-one choice of flounder anglers, but it does make an effective flattie bait.

Big fluke are aggressive predators that can be caught on a variety of live baits, including snapper bluefish, peanut bunker, spot, croaker and white perch.

FLOUNDER FINS

After you have used the baits described above to catch a limit of fluke, including a few doormats, and as you stand at the cleaning table filleting your catch and anticipating a delicious flounder dinner, make it a point to save an important part of the carcass. The long fin around the edge of a flounder makes a very good flounder bait. Trim the fins as you clean flounder, cut the fins into six to 10 inch sections, then refrigerate or freeze them until your next flounder trip. A long, fluttering ribbon of fin will provoke strikes from big flounder.

Cutting bait is a very important job, so take your time and do it right. Always use a sharp knife, and carefully cut strips from prime spots on the baitfish, such as the belly and shoulder sections. Make sure each strip is thin, with no bones or ragged edges that may cause the bait to spin instead of flutter.

When cutting strips of bluefish or croaker, you may want to leave the tail on as it will flap in the water, providing the appearance of a swimming baitfish. However, it's important to first check that the tail does not cause the bait to spin. With or without a tail, before every drop, check the rig and bait by hanging it over the side of the boat, just under the surface, where you can see it as it moves through the water. If there's any glitch in the appearance or movement of the bait or rig, either fix it or replace it. Don't waste valuable fluke fishing time with a presentation that's less than perfect.

ODDBALL BAITS THAT WORK

A surprising number of fluke are caught on live eels each year, usually by anglers who aren't even fishing for fluke. They're drifting eels in hopes of hooking striped bass, but a hungry fluke won't hesitate to attack when an eel shows up overhead. However, because of the expense and the agonizing frustration that slimy, slippery eels can inflict, most anglers choose other baits when targeting fluke.

Other baits that will trigger fluke strikes include chunks of peeler (shedder crabs), live sand fleas, strips of mackerel belly, grass shrimp, bloodworms, sandworms, live mullet and mullet strips, and even strips of chicken breast. As we said earlier in this chapter, fluke are an aggressive fish that attack and eat a wide variety of marine life!

CHAPTER 5

FOOL FLUKE WITH ARTIFICIALS

No doubt, a vast majority of flounder are caught on bait. However, it is possible, and quite enjoyable, to fish for and catch flounder on artificial lures. There's a great deal of personal satisfaction that comes with using our fishing skills to fool flounder into believing that a chunk of lead with some deer hair, or a piece of plastic, is something that looks good enough to eat!

BUCKTAILS

Generations of anglers have used a painted chunk of lead with a hook and deer hair tied on the back, to catch flounder. Bucktails continue to pass the test of time with flying colors—bucktails are still putting plenty of fluke in coolers!

While bucktails have remained basically the same over time, a few productive innovations have been introduced. Spro and other companies have incorporated modern 3-D technology to create bucktails with a realistic head that feature laser eyes and a hologram finish. Strips of Mylar tied in with the bucktail hair bring a silvery flash that's nearly identical to the flash of light reflecting off the scales of baitfish. Silver bullet or cannonball jigs, while very similar to bucktails, feature bucktail and hooks that are free to swing independently of the head, providing more motion when jigged.

The appeal of a bucktail is usually enhanced by adding a strip bait or a bloodworm to the hook. In back bay and other shallow-water fishing locations, especially when the current isn't running too hard, it may be possible to fish with a shad dart instead of a bucktail (shad darts are a mini-bucktail and are frequently used in freshwater to catch shad and crappie).

Or, a shad dart can be added to the leader or line above a bucktail to provide a teaser. A shad dart teaser can be quickly added on by tying a dropper loop 18 inches to two feet above the bucktail.

Then, right next to the dropper knot, cut one leg of the dropper loop, which will create a single piece of leader (not a loop) that stands out from the main leader. The teaser is tied to the end of the single piece that was created by cutting the leg of the loop. A common theory is that as the rig is jigged along the bottom, it appears the bucktail may be chasing the smaller teaser, which triggers the predatory instinct in flounder, prompting it to attack one of the two lures.

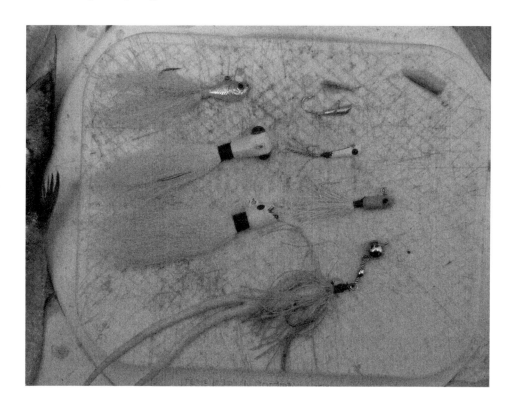

Bucktails bounced along the bottom will bring fluke to the boat.

In addition to shad darts, saltwater flies and streamers, or even a plain hook with a small soft plastic bait threaded on, also make effective teasers when tied above a bucktail.

Extra attention is needed when netting and unhooking a flounder caught on a teaser rig. It's important to remember that the rig features two hooks, one of which is exposed and can quickly bury itself in human flesh if the flounder flops or is dropped. The bucktail or shad dart hook, especially the hook not in the flounder, can also foul the net. A lot of valuable fishing time can be wasted while carefully removing the rig from the net.

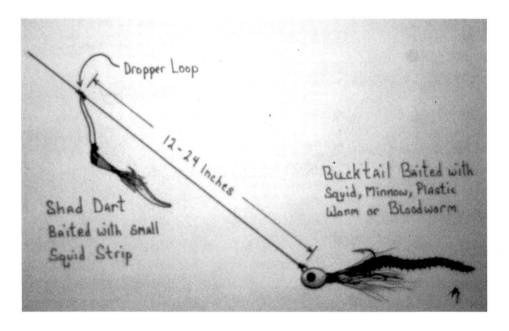

A shad dart makes a great fluke teaser when rigged on a dropper loop above a bucktail.

SOFT PLASTICS

Another fake bait for fluke is a soft plastic body or swimming tail on a leadhead jig. A few productive plastics include Bass Assassins, Berkley Power Baits, Sassy Shads, Fin-S Fish, Mister Twisters, Kalin's, Cotee baits—the list goes on and on. They are threaded on the leadhead so they are straight and will move through the water with a natural appearance. The leadhead sinks the plastic to the bottom where it can be twitched and bounced directly in the flounder's strike zone.

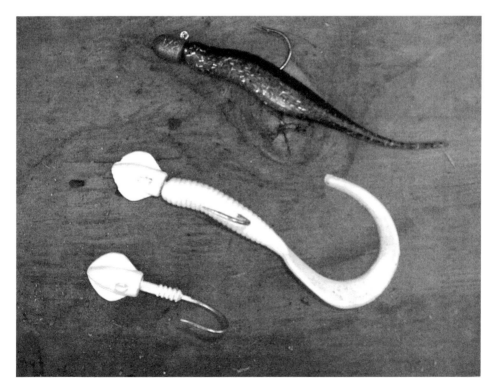

Fluke will whack soft plastics such as Bass Assassins and curly tails on a leadhead jig.

Not only do realistic soft plastic baits look, feel and move like live baitfish, worms, eels and crustaceans, many of them are impregnated with chemicals that also make them smell and taste just like the marine critters they are designed to imitate. Berkley, as an example, has been a leader in creating scented and flavored baits. All of these factors work together in tricking a flounder to strike, and in encouraging flounder to hang on longer once it has grabbed the plastic. Today's soft plastics are so incredibly realistic, with life-like profiles, motions and colors, plus natural scents and flavors, that they'll catch flounder just as they are, with no bait added. If you do hang a strip bait alongside of one, make it a small, thin strip that will in no way interfere with the motion of the plastic bait.

TECHNIQUES FOR FISHING ARTIFICIALS

Bucktails and leadheads with plastics can be fished in much the same way. If current and wind allow, drop the bucktail or leadhead to the bottom so the drifting boat pulls the lure along. The angler should use an occasional flick of the wrist to raise the rod tip and jig the lure off the bottom, then lower the rod tip so the lure falls back to the bottom. Don't just drop the rod tip; instead, lower it carefully so the line stays tight as the lure sinks. Many strikes will occur as the lure is sinking back to the bottom, and the strikes won't be detected if the lure is allowed to sink on slack line.

The drift of the boat may be too fast to keep the lure on the bottom for long. When this occurs, cast in the direction the boat is drifting, and allow the bucktail or leadhead to sink to bottom ahead of the boat. Then reel in slack, and bounce the lure by flicking the wrist to raise the rod tip. Then lower the rod tip and reel in slack. Next flick the wrist, and repeat until the lure and drifting boat come together, then cast and begin again. The boat drifting toward the lure will help keep it on the bottom where the angler can effectively jig it. The lure bouncing up and down along the bottom, plus the puffs of sand or mud it kicks up as it strikes bottom, imitate a feeding baitfish or a burrowing crab, or perhaps a baitfish that has been injured and is in its death throes.

When the drift is slow, more bottom can be covered and more flounder can be caught by casting the bucktail or leadhead away from the boat and allowing it to sink to the bottom. Then swing the rod tip horizontally at about waist level. Then reel in slack and begin again with another horizontal swing. This raises the bucktail slightly off the bottom and moves it nearly parallel to the bottom, and evidently resembles a spooked or fleeing baitfish.

In very shallow locations during periods of slow-moving water, especially early and late in the day when it's usually calm and boat traffic is very light, the best approach may be to fish a soft plastic bait with no weight at all. Thread the plastic onto a hook tied on the end of the line or leader. Cast, and slowly retrieve the weightless lure. Gently twitch the rod tip during the retrieve to make the plastic lure dive and dart like a struggling baitfish. That's a temptation most fluke are not able to resist.

METAL JIGGING LURES

Metal jigging lures such as Stingsilvers, Hopkins, Crippled Herrings, Jacky Jigs, Kastmaster spoons, Strata spoons, and others, will also elicit strikes from flounder. Most have slender profiles that enable them to cut through the water and stay on the bottom. Their sleek design also closely matches the size and shape of many baitfish species along the Mid Atlantic and North East coasts. Metal jigs feature smooth or hammered finishes, or realistic holographic patterns and other features that make them spitting images of real baitfish.

Many come equipped with a treble hook, and it's recommended that the treble be replaced with a single hook. A strip bait can be hung on the hook, if desired. Jig it on the bottom just as you would a bucktail or leadhead with a plastic, again paying close attention as the lure falls back to the bottom, when many strikes occur.

When jigged up and down on the bottom, Stingsilvers, Hopkins and similar metal lures flash and flutter, plus kick up puffs of sand and mud, attracting the attention of fluke.

CAN'T BEAT BRAID

Braided and superlines are perfect for jigging the bottom with bucktails, leadheads or metal jigging lures. Braided and superlines lines are much thinner in diameter than comparable monofilament, so they meet with little water resistance, which keeps the lure on the bottom and in the strike zone longer.

JIGGING RIGS

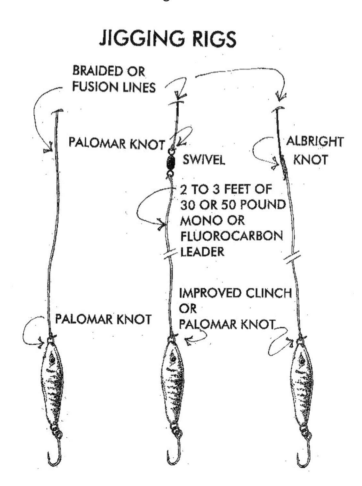

BRAIDED OR FUSION LINES

PALOMAR KNOT

SWIVEL

ALBRIGHT KNOT

2 TO 3 FEET OF 30 OR 50 POUND MONO OR FLUOROCARBON LEADER

PALOMAR KNOT

IMPROVED CLINCH OR PALOMAR KNOT

Jigging with braid requires some specific rigging techniques.

Braided lines also don't stretch, and this is important for several reasons. For starters, the absence of stretch provides incredible sensitivity, making it easy to detect strikes, even when the lure is falling back to the bottom. With the increased sensitivity, it's also easy to detect every thump of the lure striking the bottom itself; there's no doubt when the lure is on the bottom, or when it has lost contact with the bottom. In fact, braided and superlines are so sensitive that it's often possible to detect what type of bottom is being fished—sand, mud, shell or rock—just by the feel of the lure thumping the bottom. And the no-stretch feature of braided and superlines provides for instant, powerful, deep-penetrating hooksets.

Use a blood knot or an Albright knot to tie a two-foot monofilament or fluorocarbon leader to the braided line. Without a leader, the hook on a bucktail, leadhead or metal jig may catch the braided line and foul the lure. However, that doesn't seem to be a problem with a thicker mono or fluorocarbon leader.

CHAPTER 6

TIDE, CURRENT AND PRODUCTIVE FLUKE STRUCTURE

Flounder feed when the water is moving. Moving water creates rips, eddies and boils as it sweeps over and around shoals, channels, rockpiles, bridge pilings and other bottom contours and structure. Moving water carries along with it sand fleas, shrimp and other crustaceans, small baitfish, seaworms and all sorts of marine critters, providing flounder with prime time opportunities to eat. Moving water pushes our boats, giving us the drifts we need for a natural presentation of our rigs and baits. The ocean, bays and tidal rivers are "alive" when the water's moving. On the other hand, everything grinds to a halt, including the flounder bite, when the water quits moving. When the water is quiet, our catches usually consist of skates and dogfish.

Obviously, moving water is one of the most critically important factors in our fluke fishing success. One key aspect to successful flounder fishing is understanding moving water and how it affects flounder at our favorite fishing locations.

TIDES VS. CURRENTS

Many people use the word "tide" when they really mean "current", and vice versa. But they are not the same thing. Tide is the vertical, or up and down movement of water. Current is the horizontal, or sideways movement of water. Current creates turbulent water, sweeps baitfish and drifts our rigs along the bottom.

The gravitational pull of the moon (and to a lesser degree the sun) creates the tides as it moves water up and down. On an incoming or flood tide, water moves into bays and into inlets (current), raising the water level (tide). At high tide, water is at its greatest vertical point for that tidal cycle. On an outgoing or ebb tide, water moves out of bays and out of inlets (current), lowering the water level (tide). At low tide, water is at its lowest vertical point for that cycle. Typically,

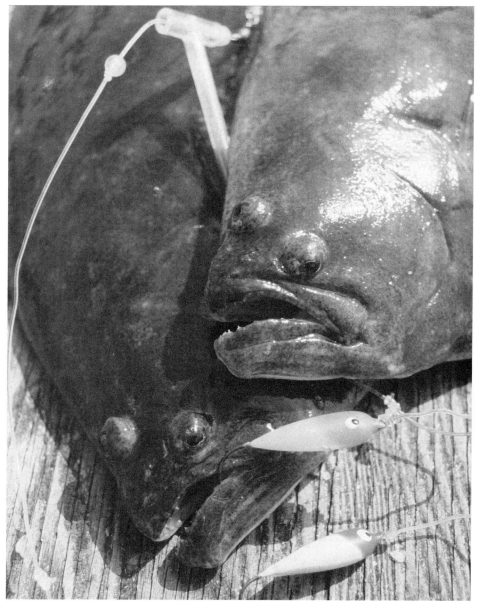

The most consistently successful fluke fishermen have a thorough
understanding of tide and current and their
impact on flounder fishing.

there are two high tides and two full tides in a day, or pretty close to it.

The current does not necessarily stop at high tide or low tide, and in fact, current can continue for quite some time after high tide and low tide. The level of the water will no longer rise or fall, but the current can continue. That means if high tide at your location is listed at 1:12 p.m. on a particular day, it may be possible to make good drifts for another half-hour, hour, or however long the current continues after 1:12 p.m.

Eventually, the current will slow and then stop, resulting in slack tide. This is when fishing suffers; there is usually little or no movement of bait, the boat probably is not drifting, and flounder won't bite. Slack water ends when the current begins to run in the opposite direction as the tide starts to rise or fall.

Depending on the time of year, wind speed and direction, and other factors, high tide in back bays, sounds and tidal rivers may enable flounder to move up and feed at locations that are inaccessible to them during an outgoing tide and low tide. They can often be caught in shallows practically at the water's edge. On the other hand, a falling tide will often pull flounder back to deeper water. There may be a very good bite as the falling tide will flush grass shrimp and other creatures out of the shallows and carry them to deeper water and waiting flounder.

Full moon periods and new moon periods can feature extremely strong currents, exceptionally high high tides, and exceptionally low low tides. Fishing can be difficult, especially in deeper water, as strong currents can make it all but impossible to keep a rig on or near the bottom.

PRODUCTIVE FLUKE STRUCTURE

If you want to catch fluke, you must fish where the fluke are—this might sound ridiculously basic and obvious, yet it's incredibly important and more involved than it may seem. A nice boat, brand new top-quality tackle, and the freshest bait will be of little benefit if you

Tom Stauffer with a beautiful 7-pound, 3-ounce doormat flounder that was 27 inches long! Flounder are caught on bottom structure such as shoals, channels, rockpiles and reefs.

don't fish where the fish are. I cannot stress enough the importance of locating and fishing structure, understanding how fluke and bait-fish relate to structure, and recognizing the impact tides and current have on where flounder will stage and how they'll feed. Fish as often as you can, and read, listen, ask questions, and write it down. Knowledge is power—the power to catch more fluke more often, and big fish consistently!

Most of the bottom in the ocean and bays is like a desert—sandy, flat, and featureless. Just like a desert, the flat featureless areas in the ocean and bays contain little or no life. In a desert, most of the life is found in an oasis, and in saltwater the "oasis" is structure. "Structure" is a general term that is used to refer to shoals (hills or uprisings on the bottom), sloughs (holes or depressions), deep-water shipping channels, bridge pilings, rockpiles, wrecks, artificial reefs, or practically any kind of depth change or irregularity in the bottom. Obviously, some structure is easy to see or find with the naked eye, including the rocky bases around lighthouses, bridge pilings, and buoys that mark the location of artificial reefs and the edges of shipping channels. When the current is strong, keep an eye out for eddies, boils and/or rips that will often form on the surface of the water over structure. Abrupt changes in water color—from green to brown, or dark green to light green, for example—may indicate the presence of bottom structure below.

For submerged, unseen structure such as shoals, sloughs, reefs and wrecks, a good chart, and a quality depthfinder and GPS, are used to pinpoint the exact locations of the structure, enabling anglers to drift or troll over it repeatedly during a day's fishing, and to return to it during future fishing trips.

There are several ways to locate and get familiar with structure in the areas you fish. Without a doubt, the best way to do it is to fish as often as you can, and keep good notes about each trip in a log book. Become an expert at reading your depthfinder and GPS and understanding the information they are providing you about the bottom.

It's also a good idea to frequent one, maybe two, tackle shops in the areas you fish. Buy your bait, tackle, ice and anything else you need at the shop(s). Become a regular. As the tackle shop operator(s) become familiar with you, he or she will be more willing to share information about the latest hot spots (structure) and how to fish them. Make friends with other fishermen and charter captains in the areas you fish, and attempt to share information with them. Attend fishing seminars and workshops. Read fishing publications such as The Fisherman magazine and others that feature how-to and where-to stories, and fishing reports, that cover the areas you fish.

A key to success is maintaining boat position over productive bottom structure.

While flounder usually gather on or near structure, they will not be spread out evenly over it. Because of current, water temperature or clarity, the availability of bait, and/or other factors, flounder will typically bunch up on a particular spot on a piece of structure. When a nice flounder is caught, immediately toss over a marker buoy to mark the spot so it's easy to return to.

SLOUGHS AND SHIPPING CHANNELS

Sloughs are similar to valleys, troughs or some sort of depression in the bottom. The edges of sloughs and shipping channels, where the bottom falls from shallow water to deeper water, are productive flounder fishing locations. Flounder position themselves on these sloping edges where they can ambush baitfish as they swim and/or hide on the edges, or while they're swept up or down the edges by the current. At times flounder can be caught on the very bottom of a slough or channel, however, they're usually found along the edges. Your time will usually be better spent drifting or trolling the

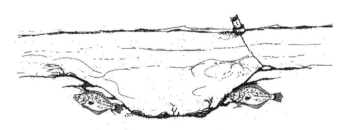

SLOUGH OR CHANNEL

**Fish for fluke on the sloping edges of sloughs
and shipping channels.**

edges rather than the deepest part of the slough or channel. Abrupt changes in the channel tend to aggregate the fish, and are spots you'll want to pay special attention to.

On a rising tide, look for flounder along the upper, shallower parts of channel edges or slough edges. Baitfish and flounder may even move up and out of the channel or slough, and into the surrounding shallower areas, as the incoming tide covers those areas with more water. During a falling tide, baitfish and flounder will drop down to the lower, deeper parts of channel edges or slough edges.

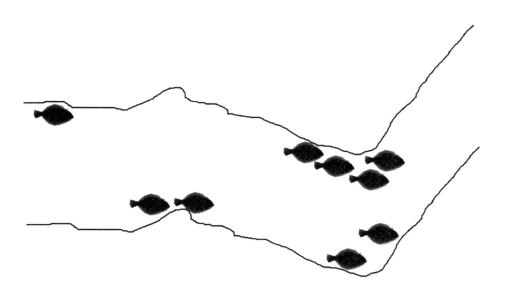

Flounder can be found along channel edges, and will group up at abrupt changes in the channel.

When a flounder or two is caught, note the depth, and make every effort to drift over that same depth for as long as possible. The most productive depth may change during the day as current and tidal conditions change.

At times, tidal, current and wind conditions will be just right, and you can make long drifts over channel edges while remaining constantly in the most productive depths. At other times, when conditions are not as favorable, you'll be required to make short drifts, frequently re-positioning the boat to keep it in the most productive depths.

Buoys often mark the edges of shipping channels—great locations for fluke fishing.

SHOALS

Shoals are humps or hill-like uprisings on the bottom. They're prime locations for not only fluke, but also stripers and our other favorite predators. In a moving current, water rushing up and over a shoal will carry with it small baitfish and crustaceans, which, in a strong current, often are not strong enough to swim in or escape the turbulent water. They tumble along, and are attacked and devoured by opportunistic fluke.

Start your drift well up-current of the shoal, and thoroughly cover the shoal with each drift—rigs should bounce up the shoal, across the top, and down the other side. When fishing shallow shoals, never run the boat directly over the shoal, as motor noise may cause fish to stop biting, at least temporarily. Instead, after finishing up one drift, re-start the motor and run around the shoal to position the boat up-current for another drift. This is usually more important when striper fishing on shoals, but why chance it with fluke?

Flounder often change their staging area on shoals as current

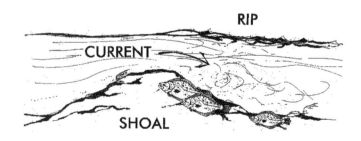

Fluke feed on shoals and other lumps and bumps on the bottom.

and water conditions change. Fish the entire structure until a specific hot spot is located, then fish that location thoroughly. When the bite begins to slow, start fishing the entire shoal again until another productive spot is located.

Large shoals are marked on charts, and can be found with a GPS and/or depthfinder. Often, during a strong current, "rips" will form on the surface of the water either directly over or just down-current of a shoal. Rips are areas of disturbed water, ranging from ripples to big waves, that are created on the surface as the current churns and tumbles water up and over a shoal. "Drifting the rips" is a common technique among striper anglers, and rips are also productive locations for flounder fishermen.

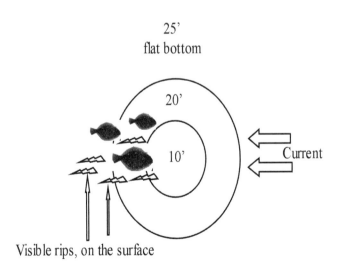

25'
flat bottom

20'

10'

Current

Visible rips, on the surface

A bird's eye view: The visible rip usually forms just behind the shoal.

BRIDGE PILINGS

Current washing around bridge pilings often scours holes and pockets in the bottom, which become fantastic hiding spots for fluke. They'll hunker down in these holes, and attack small fish and crabs as they swim, or are washed in the current, over the holes.

Often, there's more structure than meets the eye at the bases of bridge pilings. Boulders or concrete are sometimes used to reinforce the supports where they enter the bottom of the river, bay or ocean. While bridges are being built, construction material may fall, or be thrown, into the water. This stuff can pile up and create a mini artificial reef that provides hiding places for baitfish, and terrific ambush locations for fluke.

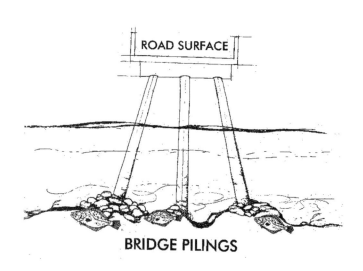

BRIDGE PILINGS

Bridge pilings can be fluke hot spots. Holes scoured in the bottom, and also rocks and concrete at the bases of bridge pilings, often hold big fluke.

Obviously, the goal is to fish near bridge pilings while avoiding any boat or motor contact with them. Leave the motor in gear, with someone constantly at the helm, for a controlled drift that will carry the boat past the piling without banging into it.

Another tactic is for the person at the wheel to position the boat up-current of the piling, with the bow pointing away from the piling and directly into the current. They should give it just enough gas to hold the boat in place. Then an angler in the back of the boat can lower their rig over the transom and to the bottom. They should occasionally play out line so the rig bounces along the bottom as the current pushes it back toward the piling.

INLETS AND JETTIES

While safety is always priority one on the water, fishing inlets requires anglers to be especially safety conscious. Big boats running through inlets can kick up large waves, a hard-running current can create turbulent water and treacherous boating conditions, and constant attentiveness is required to keep the boat from drifting into other boats, jetty boulders or bridge pilings. However, when fished safely and correctly, inlets can produce some outstanding catches of big fluke.

It's the funneling affect of water through an inlet that can make them difficult, yet also productive, to fish. On an incoming tide, water from the ocean is funneled through a narrow inlet, while an outgoing tide funnels water from tidal rivers and back bays through the inlet. This churning, tumbling water sweeps along bait, and creates rips and eddies on the surface as it swirls over and past bottom structure, jetty rocks, and bridge pilings. Search out these fish-attracting locations within an inlet, and drift over and around them with strip baits, live baits and artificial lures.

Exactly when an inlet will be most productive depends on the season, the tide and other factors. Following are just several examples of when fluke in an inlet will be most aggressively feeding.

In the summer and early fall, when the water in shallow back bays

Anglers drifting in inlets, and fishermen casting from jetties, hook up with nice flounder.

and tidal rivers is very warm, an incoming tide may trigger a good fluke bite as the current brings cooler water from the ocean through the inlet and into back bays.

In the spring and late fall, an outgoing tide may be most productive. During high tide, the sun may have warmed the water in relatively shallow back bay areas. It may only be one or two degrees warmer than the water in the inlet and ocean, but that may be all that's needed to put fluke on the feed during an outgoing tide as the warmer water is funneled through the inlet.

At any time of the year, at high tide, water will flood onto flats and marshy areas. As the outgoing tide begins, the falling water will flush minnows and other small baitfish, crabs and critters from the shallows and through the inlet. This swirling buffet offers fluke a fantastic opportunity to fatten up. Fish your favorite inlet(s) frequently, keep good notes in a log book, and soon you'll see a pattern develop as to when and where fluke bite best.

Inlet jetties can be good places to hook up with nice fluke if you don't have a boat, too, since it's possible to walk out onto many of them. But do not venture out onto the rocks without a pair of Korkers or golf cleats. Those boulders are slipperier than they appear, and fishermen without the proper footwear are risking a nasty, dangerous and perhaps even life-threatening spill. And while we're on the topic of jetty fashion, other items that are strongly recommended include good raingear, both tops and bottoms, for protection against breaking waves and wind; knee-high boots (with Korkers over top of them); a hat or visor; and polarized sunglasses. A vest works well for carrying sinkers, rigs, bucktails, nail clippers and a rag. Wear several layers of light clothing for warmth and mobility, and keep a complete change of dry clothing in the truck in case of an accidental soaking.

Bucktails and long strip baits on a sliding egg sinker rig get a lot of work among jetty anglers. Cast and slowly retrieve them so they move along the bottom, just as they would from a drifting boat. Flounder may be out in the middle of the inlet, or up tight against the jetty rocks, or anywhere in between, so cover each spot along a jetty by fan casting. Fan cast both the inlet side and the ocean side

An early-spring flounder hooked on a chilly afternoon during an out-going tide, which provided the warmest water of the day.

of a jetty. There may even be flounder right at your feet; don't be sur-
prised to hook a fish just as you were about to lift the rig or bucktail
from the water for another cast. Remember, flounder bunch up, so
when a fish is caught, make the same cast over and over again to
catch other fish that may be at that spot. Look for spots along the
jetty where there are holes or rocks out of place, to gather concentra-
tions of the fish.

Instead of casting and retrieving, you can also cast the bucktail or rig up-current and allow the moving water to push it along the
bottom. Slowly pick up any slack line as the rig or bucktail is swept
past. When it gets down-current, retrieve and cast again, this time a
little farther or a little closer to the rocks, so the rig or bucktail is swept
over a new stretch of bottom. Fish all along a jetty, including out and

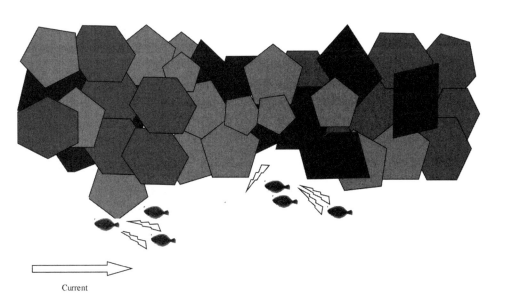

Current

**Any unusual change in the jetty which causes a shift in the current
flow can attract the fish.**

around the end. You never know when your bucktail or rig is going to drop into a depression or find another hot spot that's loaded with nice fluke.

WRECKS AND REEFS

Hundreds of "Red Bird" subway cars from New York City Transit, a 90-foot tug boat, plus a Navy barge, dozens of tanks and armored personnel carriers were all sunk 16.5 nautical miles off Indian River Inlet to create Delaware's Artificial Reef Site 11. The 1.3 square mile site is in 68 to 88 feet of water. Jeff Tinsman, Director of the Delaware Artificial Reef Program, has spotted some big fluke while diving on the site. One interesting observation has been doormat fluke lying directly on top of the subway cars, some 10 feet above the ocean bottom.

There are wrecks and reefs like this one all along the Northeast and Mid Atlantic coasts, and they are popular fishing locations for anglers hoping to hook tautog (blackfish), sea bass, cod, pollock and spadefish. Fluke also hang out in and around these hard structure areas. That's because they're often inhabited by smaller fish that use them for hiding places and protection. Flounder are often caught on the sandy or mud bottom areas right next to wrecks and reefs, where they conceal themselves and wait for the opportunity to ambush smaller fish that happen to venture just a little too far outside of the structure. And as Tinsman's diving experiences have shown us, fluke will also hide directly on and in reefs and wrecks.

When your boat arrives at the lat/long coordinates for a wreck or reef, mark that spot by tossing over a marker buoy. If the structure is not immediately seen on the depthfinder, start slowly circling the marker buoy while keeping an eye on the depthfinder. Start by making small circles around the buoy, then gradually enlarge the circles until you find the structure. Then toss over a second marker buoy or enter the spot on the GPS. Slowly motor the boat over the location several times while watching the depthfinder to determine how the wreck or reef is positioned on the bottom.

It's possible to drift over and around wrecks and reefs with live bait, strip baits, or bucktails. However, they'll be short drifts; a lot of time will be spent re-positioning the boat for the next drift. Drifts need to be short and precise so they carry the boat directly over the structure, or right alongside it. Do not waste time drifting and fishing open bottom once you've moved off of the structure. When the boat is no longer over it, it's time to motor up-current and start the next drift. Snags can become a frequent and frustrating problem, and to reduce the number of snags anglers need to constantly jig and bounce their offerings, and keep them up and out of the structure.

Some anglers prefer to anchor over a wreck or reef and fish it with live bait, or cast with a bucktail, or a soft plastic (Bass Assassin and others) on a leadhead jig. The bait or lure will make lots of con-

Concrete culvert and other material towed out to sea are dumped overboard to create an artificial reef.

tact with the structure, so it's very important to frequently check the leader and line and immediately replace them if there are any nicks or abrasion.

One wreck and reef anchoring technique involves running directly up-current of the marker buoy over the wreck or reef, dropping anchor, and paying out line until the boat drifts back to the buoy. Then, the line is secured to a bow cleat.

Others use rebar anchors, which are made from metal bars used to reinforce concrete. The boat is moved up-current of the wreck or reef, the anchor is dropped over and the drifting boat pulls the anchor along the bottom until the rebar hooks or snags the structure. Then the anchor line is tied off to the bow cleat with as little scope as possible, so the boat sits directly over the structure (anchor like this on only calm days).

Productive fluke wrecks can be located on nautical charts that are available in many tackle shops and most marine stores. Wreck locations have also been published in a number of fishing books, including Rudow's Guide to Fishing the Mid Atlantic, another book produced by Geared Up Publications. (This book includes over 300 hotspots in coastal bays, inlets, inshore, and even offshore waters, from New York to North Carolina.) Both charts and books usually feature the latitude and longitude of the wrecks so they can be located with a GPS. Some fishing-related websites also provide the names of wrecks and their locations.

For the exact locations of man-made artificial reefs, and information about what they're made of, contact your state's artificial reef program, or the Fish and Game Division in your state's Department of Natural Resources or Department of Environmental Conservation (see chapter one for website addresses and phone numbers). For instance, Delaware's Artificial Reef Program each year publishes updated information about all of its reefs, and it will mail the reef guide, at no charge, to anyone who requests it.

PIERS

Piers are fantastic fluke fishing platforms. Plenty of fluke, and lots of big ones, are caught each season by anglers walking the boards and fishing over the rails. Because the water around most piers is relatively shallow, a lightweight rig usually works very well. Tie a 1/0 or 2/0 wide-gap hook directly onto the end of the mono from the reel, and about three feet above the hook put on a light rubber-core sinker.

Another effective rig features a small egg sinker. The line from the reel is threaded through the sinker, then through one or two plastic beads, and then a small barrel swivel is tied on to the end of the line. A three-foot leader of 20 pound fluorocarbon, with the hook at

Lots of fluke are caught by anglers fishing on foot (not in boats). Piers, docks, canals, and back-bay areas are easily-accessible and highly-productive fluke fishing locations.

the other end, is then tied to the swivel. Productive baits include a live minnow with a strip of squid. With either one of these rigs, cast away from the pier and slowly retrieve it.

On a pier when it's not crowded, I recommend taking your rig for a walk. Drop the rig straight down to the bottom and then slowly walk along the rail, jigging the bait as you go. This enables your bait to cover bottom in search of fluke, just as it would in a drifting boat. Be especially prepared for strikes as your bait moves past the pilings. Big fluke hang out near pilings, as small baitfish use the pilings as hiding spots. Also, the current will often scour depressions at the base of pier pilings, and fluke love to lay in those depressions and ambush prey as it swims overhead. I have caught several flounder, one right after the other, from the same depression.

Piers with lights can feature exciting fluke fishing opportunities when the sun goes down. After dark, baitfish will swarm under pier lights shining on the water. Fluke will often position themselves where the light begins to fade and the water begins to darken, an area commonly called the "light line." They can be caught on the same rigs and baits that are used in the daytime, or, this is prime time for catching fluke on artificials. Cast out and slowly retrieve a light leadhead jig dressed with a soft plastic bait. Note that the leadhead-and-plastic combo should closely match the size of the prevalent baitfish hanging out under the lights. Occasionally stop bringing in line so the leadhead sinks to the bottom, then resume the slow retrieve.

On the near-shore part of a pier, which is often over water so shallow that the light shines through the water the whole way to the bottom, it may be possible to watch your rig or leadhead as it's retrieved, and to see fluke dart up off the bottom and grab it!

Piers can be particularly productive fluke fishing hot spots in the spring. The water in the ocean and bays is still very cool early in the season, but shallow-water areas along the shoreline (where piers are) are usually a few degrees warmer. That's especially true at high tide in the afternoons when the sun is high and skies are clear and bright. The sun shining down on shallow water will warm it up, which attracts baitfish, and brings in bigger predators. Fluke will often set up near a pier, especially at the beginning of an outgoing tide when the current will pull baitfish from the shallows toward deeper water.

FLOUNDER UNDER FEATHERS

It's a sight that never fails to trigger an adrenaline rush: baitfish splashing on the surface, under attack from fish below and birds from above. In a frantic attempt to escape rampaging stripers, bluefish, false albacore and other predators that are devouring them from below, baitfish dash to the surface and attempt to hide in the waves or even jump clear of the water. But there they often come under an aerial assault, as screaming gulls and terns dive to the surface to feast on the baitfish, or at least pick up the pieces. Life is difficult, and often short, for small baitfish in saltwater!

While we can have a blast catching stripers, bluefish and false albacore in these situations, be aware that topwater activity and working birds often mean that big flounder are also in the vicinity. They'll hang out below fish that are devastating baitfish on the surface, feeding on the dead and injured bait as it sinks to the bottom. It's easy pickings, and fluke take full advantage of it.

The key is to cast into the melee, not pull your boat into the middle of it. You do not want to cause the stripers, bluefish or albacore to sound and the baitfish and birds to disappear, ending the exciting fishing opportunity before you have fully enjoyed it. Instead, motor up alongside the topwater commotion, taking care not to get too close or spook the fish. Cast a bucktail tipped with a strip of squid or cut bait into the panicked baitfish. Allow it to sink to the bottom, and then gently jig the bucktail by raising and lowering the rod tip. Or, retrieve it very slowly so it drags across the bottom. This will kick up puffs of sand or mud, much like a dying fish, and fluke will be quick to pounce.

Make sure you're prepared to seize the moment the next time you see baitfish boiling on the surface, and birds working above them. Our feathered friends may be showing you exactly where you can hook your next big fluke.

CHAPTER 7

DRIFTING, TROLLING, ANCHORING, AND PARTY BOAT FLOUNDER

Fluke feed when the current is running and bait is on the move. Fluke attack fish, crustaceans and worms as they swim, hop or crawl on or near the bottom, or as they move along in the current. The key is movement, and fluke anglers in boats either drift or troll to present moving baits to fluke. There are times when it may pay to anchor, and jig and/or cast, and anchoring is covered in this book; however, most fluke are caught while drifting or trolling.

DRIFTING

Drifting is a very popular approach. However, leisurely drifting along, while haphazardly dragging a bait across the bottom, with only a half-hearted interest in the bottom structure and water depth, just won't cut it! Consistently successful drifting is a hands-on and dynamic process. Careful planning, concentration, and actively controlling the speed and direction of the boat are all key ingredients to productive drifting.

Successful drifting begins well before the boat rolls off the trailer. Before each trip, it's important to review log books from previous fishing seasons; to obtain recent fluke fishing reports from friends, bait and tackle shop operators, the Internet, and/or magazines; and to consult charts of the area you'll be fishing. Develop a plan as to exactly which structure will be fished, and during which particular tidal stage each piece of structure will be fished.

When you hit the water, use the GPS, compass and/or chart to run directly to the first structure to be fished. Upon arrival, take a few moments to study the current and wind, and carefully position the boat for the first drift.

Mark the starting point of the first drift by tossing over a marker buoy, or entering the location into the GPS. That way, if the drift is productive, it's easy to return to that exact spot to drift again, over that same piece of productive bottom. If no fluke are caught on the first drift, pick up the marker buoy and use a different starting point so new bottom will be fished during the second drift (drop the buoy at each new starting point). When a nice fluke is hooked, mark that

Watching the depthfinder, re-positioning the boat over structure, as necessary, and keeping baits in the strike zone are key ingredients to successful drifting and will trigger strikes like this one!

particular spot with another buoy so several short drifts can be made over it. Once that spot has been worked over, retrieve the buoys and set up for the next drift.

During each and every drift, it's critically important to keep close watch on the depthfinder. It's imperative that the drift be maintained in the most productive depth, or over the exact part of the structure that's expected to hold the most fluke. It may be necessary to occasionally start the motor and bump it in and out of gear to nudge the boat to where it needs to be. If the wind pushes the boat too far off the drift, anglers will need to pick up their lines so the boat can be re-positioned. It may be necessary to move the boat several times during one drift. But make the effort–do not waste valuable fishing time by allowing the boat to drift over unproductive bottom. By staying sharp, focused and active, you'll increase your chances of limiting out and catching doormat fluke.

The direction and speed of the current and wind, and the size of the boat, are among the most important factors that affect drifting. Ideal fishing conditions usually feature a light breeze blowing in the same direction as the current. This will move the boat and the baits naturally with the current, while providing strip baits with a tantalizing fluttering action.

Unfortunately, as we're all well aware, conditions are not always ideal. Too often we encounter wind blowing against or across the current, or wind with the current that results in rapid drifting conditions. Don't just sit back and subject yourself to unfavorable and unproductive conditions, instead, fight back, take action, and try to put the odds in your favor.

One way to slightly change your drift begins by checking your motor. Turning it one way or the other may improve the direction, or the boat's positioning, during the drift. Raising the motor out of the water may result in a better drift. Or, leaving it in the water, and occasionally starting it and bumping it in and out of gear, may help the boat fight the wind while holding the boat directly above the structure. Some anglers install a smaller "kicker" motor or electric trolling motor on their boat, to be used for a controlled drift.

A sea anchor (drogue,) a parachute-like device which you secure to a cleat and pull through the water, can be used to slow a drifting boat in the strong currents during new moon and full moon periods, or if the wind is strong and blowing in the same direction as the current. If you don't have a sea anchor a five-gallon bucket makes a pretty good alternative. Tie a length of rope to the bucket handle, tie off the other end of the rope to a boat cleat, and toss the bucket overboard. The bucket will quickly fill with water, and as it is dragged through the water it will slow the boat. Where the drogue is tied off in the boat will determine the boat's positioning as it drifts. If necessary,

A five-gallon bucket tied off to a cleat can help slow a boat that's drifting too fast for effective fishing, especially when fishing deeper water.

try several spots until the boat is just right for most effective fishing. Say, for example, the drogue is cleated off on the bow, and causing the boat to drift stern-first with the current. Since the current is really ripping, it's carrying your lines directly back, from the stern. This situation would be fine if there were only one or two anglers aboard. But if there are four of you and only enough room for two at the stern, fishing is tough. You can improve this situation by cleating the drogue off of an amidships spring cleat. By moving the tension from the bow to amidships the boat will swing beam-to with the current, and now, all the anglers aboard have plenty of room to fish.

Other ways to slow a boat include keeping a low profile. Lower everything–Bimini tops, canvas, antenna, rods, flags–that may be catching wind and increasing boat speed. Anglers should fish sitting down. (Chapter eight features very interesting and useful information on effective drifting and maintaining proper boat position directly over productive structure, especially when the wind is blowing across the current. It describes how to fish with the stern of the boat into the wind, bumping the motor into reverse when necessary to fight the wind.)

Conversely, if there is no wind and current, or the wind is against the current, therefore causing little or no drift, you may be able to get a drift going by increasing sail area; put up your Bimini top, for example. At times, when the conditions require, you will need to create your own boat movement by bumping the motor in and out of gear. Cover as much bottom as possible until the current kicks in again. If a fluke is hooked, shut off the motor and jig that spot with a two-hook high-low rig, or a bucktail, since the lack of motion means you'll remain planted over the hotspot.

As we stated earlier, there's a lot that goes into successful fluke drifting. Thinking, decision-making and action are not optional—they are required! Productive drifting is not a lazy man's game. Electronics–depthfinder and GPS–are incredibly important tools for drifting (and trolling). A depthfinder enables us to visualize the bottom and the presence of baitfish, plus it provides surface water temperature and other useful information. Entering the lat/long into the

GPS for the structures to be fished makes it possible to run right to them, drift after drift, trip after trip, season after season. GPS and GPS/depthfinder combination units with charting abilities also provide additional details, such as the exact current boat location on

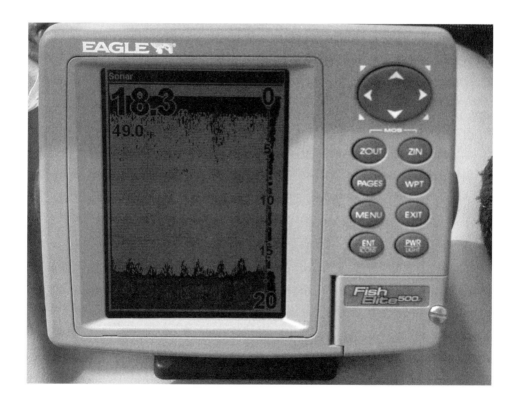

A depthfinder provides a visual of the bottom contours and structure.

an electronic chart, including the boat's position in relation to bottom structure and contours. They will also mark the exact path of each drift, so each successful drift can be repeated. Electronics make us more efficient and effective fishermen.

GPS units with charting abilities mark the exact boat position over contours, as well as the path of a drift or trolling pattern, so it can be repeated, ensuring the boat once again travels over the precise piece of productive bottom.

DRIFTING ROCKPILES

Underwater rocks and boulders are fantastic fluke fishing locations. Many of the biggest doormats caught each season come from rockpiles. However, working rockpiles can be challenging and frustrating. A certain amount of experience and know-how are required before rockpiles can be fished effectively on a consistent basis.

Much of my rockpile fishing experience has been at the Chesapeake Bay Bridge Tunnel at the mouth of the Chesapeake Bay in Virginia. Several expert fluke anglers have shown me how to fish the rocks, and their tips and tactics can be used to successfully target barndoor fluke on rockpiles from New England to North Carolina.

As the nearly 20-mile long Chesapeake Bay Bridge Tunnel complex was being constructed across the mouth of the bay, tons and tons of huge boulders were dumped on top of the two tunnel portions of the complex. While the bridge sections carry cars and trucks above the water, vehicles in the tunnels are actually driving along the bottom of the bay. There are two "openings" in the complex where the tunnels go to the bottom, and large container ships and huge military vessels use these openings to sail freely in and out of the bay (those ships are just too big to fit under the bridge sections of the complex). However, the boulders do much more than stabilize the tunnels, they're also hot spots for fluke anglers hoping to hook up with trophy fish.

Baits can be drifted over, or trolled along, the submerged boulders. No matter which approach is used, specialized tackle and techniques are needed.

Snags are nuisance number one when drifting rockpiles. It's just too easy for a sinker to get wedged in all those crevices among boulders. To reduce hang-ups, rockpile experts let out just enough line to get their rig straight down to the bottom. The sinker must be heavy enough to pull the rig straight down and keep it there while the boat drifts over the rocks.

As the boat drifts from upcurrent to directly over the boulders, the angler needs to be raising and lowering the rod tip. Fishing straight up and down, and frequently raising the rod tip and lifting the rig, will help keep it out of the rocks. Every second or third time the rod tip is lowered, the angler should feel the falling sinker thump against the rocks. Claude Bain, Director of the Virginia Saltwater Fishing Tournament and one of the experts I have fished with on the rocks, describes this as "playing tag with the bottom," or "walking a bait." The goal is to keep the rig and the bait moving right along the tops of the rocks where the flounder are, while keeping the sinker from falling into the cracks and crevices.

It takes heavy, tough tackle to effectively fish rockpiles, whether they're at the Chesapeake Bay Bridge Tunnel, or elsewhere. At the Chesapeake Bay Bridge Tunnel, water depths on top of the rocks are 30 to 40 feet, while the surrounding depths are 45 to 60 feet. At times, the current screams over the submerged boulders, and heavy sinkers of 10 ounces, or even more, will be needed to keep the rig straight down from the boat. Timing can be crucial, as you'll want to avoid peak current times, if possible. It sometimes roars through here so strongly, that it's nearly impossible to fish effectively. Try to plan your trip so you're on the water and in position to fish at the very beginning or end of an incoming or outgoing tide, when the current just begins to move, or starts to slow down before going slack.

This type of fishing is most easily and effectively accomplished with conventional levelwind reels on sturdy, fast-action rods. Braided lines are also recommended for several reasons: because their thin diameter meets with less water resistance, the lines cut through the water and keep rigs down near the bottom; their lack of stretch and increased sensitivity make it possible to feel every thump of the sinker bouncing on the boulders (there's no doubt the rig is on the bottom); and their super sensitivity makes the angler instantly aware of every fluke bite, even when it's in the 45 to 60 foot depths just off the rockpiles.

A palomar knot is used to tie a three-way swivel to the end of the braided line from the reel. To the bottom eye of the swivel, tie on about a foot of monofilament, with a loop tied in the other end of the mono to hold the sinker. On the final eye of the three-way swivel, a clinch knot is used tie on a two-foot piece of 50 pound test fluorocarbon leader. While many anglers fish this rig with only a piece of strip bait, others prefer to add some color and additional attraction in the form of yellow or chartreuse hair teasers, or plastic squid bodies, which are slipped on the leader just ahead of the hook. You may want to put one or two beads on the leader, both in front of and behind the bucktail teaser or squid. (See the rockpile drifting rig diagram in chapter two.)

Top baits for rockpile rigs include long, narrow strip baits cut from freshly-caught bluefish, croaker (hardhead), sea robins, and sand sharks (smooth dogfish), and also long squid strips. Strip baits should be at least six inches long, and even eight and 10 inch strips will trigger strikes from hungry doormat fluke. Baits should not be cut pennant-shaped in this situation, as the wider front end of a pennant-shaped bait may cause it to spin unnaturally as the rig is drifted over the rocks in the tremendous current. Instead, strip baits should be cut so they're about the same width throughout, from beginning to end. They'll move through the water naturally, with a come-hither fluttering action that fluke often cannot resist.

Now that we're rigged up, the bait's cut and we're ready to go, let's take a look at the typical rockpile drifting procedure. Position the boat on the up-current side of the submerged boulders, which at the Chesapeake Bay Bridge Tunnel puts you in 45 to 60 feet of water. Disengage the spool and allow the rig to sink to the bottom, using your thumb to stop the spool the instant the rig hits bottom. Any extra slack should be reeled in so the line goes straight down from the rod tip, with the rig straight down from the boat.

Raise and lower the rod tip as the boat drifts toward the rocks. If you can't feel the sinker hitting the rocks, reel up and put on a heavier sinker. Do not let out more line when contact with the bottom is lost, because that means the rig will be farther away from the boat (no longer straight up and down), which means the sinker will soon be dragged into the rocks and snagged.

As the boat begins to drift over the rocks on the tunnel, the water will get shallower, the sinker will bang bottom more frequently, and it will be necessary to reel in the extra line so the rig remains straight up and down. Continue to reel in line as needed as the rig is bounced over the boulders to the top of the rockpile, where the water will be 30 to 40 feet deep.

Next comes the only point in the rockpile drifting process where it's necessary to let out line. As the boat drifts over the top of the rocks and begins moving over the down-current side of the boulders, the water will begin to get deeper, making it necessary to let out a little line at a time to remain in contact with the bottom. Continue drifting, and occasionally pay out a little line, until the boat has moved off the rockpile. Then it's time to start the motor and run back to the up-current starting point for another drift over the boulders.

If you're new to rockpile drifting, it will take a little time to develop the feel necessary to determine the difference between a fluke grabbing the bait, and the sinker striking rocks. When there's a fluke on, point the rod tip directly at the fish, which will provide slack for just a moment before the drifting boat pulls the line tight again. Then set the hook and begin working the fish up and off the rocks.

TROLLING

Trolling is a great way to put moving, tempting baits directly in front of hungry fluke. Trolling provides for better boat control, enabling the angler to keep the boat over structure, and baits in the strike zone, for sustained periods of time. Trolling can also effectively cover bottom and locate fluke when they're spread out. Once a nice fluke is caught, the angler can choose to troll, drift or anchor on that particular piece of productive bottom. Trolling can be just the ticket for a limit catch when wind and/or current conditions will not allow for effective drifting.

Just like drifting, thorough preparation for successful trolling begins at least a day or two before the actual fishing trip. Review log books from previous weeks and previous fishing seasons, and consult your friends, your local tackle shop, and/or the Internet and fishing publications for the latest fishing reports from the area you will be fishing. Where have fluke been caught recently, during which tidal stage, and on which baits? Look at a chart, and plan exactly where you will troll, and when. A plan should be in place by the time you hit the water.

A lot of big fluke are caught each season while trolling channel edges and other productive bottom contours.

When trolling, the boat needs to move slowly enough so the sinkers and rigs maintain steady contact with the bottom, yet the boat needs to move quickly enough so that the baits bounce and flutter enticingly over the bottom. Don't be afraid to give the boat a little gas, and if necessary, use sinkers as heavy as 12, 18 and even 20 ounces, even in relatively shallow water, to hold bottom. Flounder are aggressive predators, and the baitfish they ambush are quick swimmers, so keep the boat and your baits moving.

Flounder are not very spooky or boat shy, and even motor noise doesn't seem to bother them. I have seen flounder caught directly behind the boat, right in the prop wash, just as the trolling boat passed over the fish. They hide by holding tight to the bottom, partially covered with mud or sand, even as big menacing bluefish and sharks cruise around. And flounder will hold tight to the bottom even as a boat passes overhead, and they'll immediately jump up and grab a bait as it's trolled by.

Thin no-stretch braided line works well when trolling, as it cuts through the water with little resistance and helps keeps rigs on the bottom. This is also an advantage wire or monel line has, and these lines also work well when trolling for flatfish. It's possible to troll with monofilament, yet water resistance on thicker monofilament tends to push the mono up, and lift rigs off the bottom. Long strip baits cut from fresh bluefish, croaker and squid are recommended for trolling. Use six, eight, and even 10 inch strips on two-hook high/low rigs, or three-way swivel rigs. Avoid live baits, or whole dead baits, as they may spin when trolled.

The key is to troll over and around shoals channel edges rockpiles and other fluke structure. It's important to keep in mind the impact current direction and speed, and wind direction and speed, will have on the boat and the presentation of the rigs and baits. Less boat speed is usually needed when trolling with the current and wind, as they will assist the motor in moving the boat. Trolling against or into the wind and current slows the boat, so more gas will be needed to keep the baits bouncing along the bottom.

When trolling across the current, especially when trolling near

The owner of this boat has it all rigged up for successful trolling. Note the kicker motor on the stern, the nearby rod holders (including the rod holder on the big motor), and the depthfinder rigged in the corner of the stern where it can be easily seen while running the kicker motor.

a shoal, wreck or rockpile, the boat should pass slightly up-current of the structure so the current pushes the rigs and baits toward the structure. But remember that flounder may be positioned on the down-current side of the structure, so begin trolling on the up-current side and make several passes until the up-current side, the top, and the down-current side of the structure have all been worked over well.

While I don't backtroll, I have fished with flounder experts who do backtroll, and believe me, it works. They troll with the motor in reverse, with the transom in the lead. It's especially effective when a slower boat speed is needed, as the transom pushing against the current and/or wind will significantly slow the boat. Novices should not attempt backtrolling in big waters, however. There is a certain amount of danger inherent in moving a boat backwards through the seas, and large waves may wash over the transom. So don't try this tactic unless you know your boat well, and are in relatively calm conditions.

It's possible to troll up big fluke on rockpiles. A sturdy, fast-action rod, and a conventional levelwind reel spooled with 40-pound test braided or wire line, which slices through the water and keeps the three-way swivel rig down deep on the bottom, are needed for successful rockpile trolling. The mono leader from the three-way swivel to hold a 12 to 20 ounce sinker is about three feet long, and the 50 pound fluorocarbon leader from the swivel to the hook is about 20 feet long. (Refer back to chapter two, for a diagram of a rockpile trolling rig). Long strip baits are used when trolling.

The boat is motored very slowly, parallel to the rockpile, on the up-current side of the boulders. Slightly angling the bow of the boat away from the rockpile and into the on-coming current will help slow the boat and slow the troll, and it will help push the long-leadered hook and bait toward and over the rockpile.

Fluke trollers often keep the reel in free spool and control the spool and line by applying pressure to the spool with their thumb. When the sinker quits striking bottom, they lift the thumb for a moment to quickly play out just enough line to get the sinker back down on the bottom.

To drop-back when there's a bite, simply lower the rod tip, which will provide enough slack for the fluke to begin swallowing the bait. As the moving boat pulls the slack tight, the rod should be sharply raised and the angler should start reeling.

Claude Bain provided this important nugget of fluke trolling advice: Always troll from shallow water to deeper water, as this will cut down on the number of snags. It's quicker and easier to let out a little line when going from shallow to deep, than it is to reel in line while trolling from deep to shallow.

Nice flounder will jump on strip baits trolled on submerged rockpiles.

ANCHORING UP TO CHUM, OR FISH A WRECK

Chumming works for stripers, bluefish, seatrout and cobia, and fluke will also make their way up a chum slick in search of a meal. It's the predatory instinct–fluke can't help but take notice when tempting scent and delicious bits and pieces drift by in the current. It tells them that something is happening up-current, and there may be a meal in it for them. They'll follow their nostrils up the chum slick and to the awaiting baits!

Current is crucial. Instead of using the current and/or wind to move the boat and the baits, current is needed to move and disperse the chum. Instead of covering bottom while drifting or trolling, the boat remains stationary and the goal is to entice the fluke to come to you. It works. In fact, my fishing buddies and I have hooked nice fluke while we were chumming for cobia, not flatfish. We were anchored up and chumming at the Cabbage Patch near Cape Charles, Virginia. Several fluke were attracted to the bunker baits that were being fished on the bottom on fish-finder rigs. The flounder just couldn't resist and were hooked as they swallowed the bunker heads and hefty shoulder sections hooked on 7/0 and 9/0 hooks!

Anchor, chum and fish near typical fluke structure, such as channels, shoals, wrecks or reefs. Since chumming can disperse scent and flavor a long way from the boat, and bring in fluke from considerable distances, even anchoring on a relatively open bottom may produce fish, yet whenever possible, chum near structure. Anchor up-current of the structure so the current carries the chum back over it, where it will whet the appetite of fluke and get them moving toward the baits.

Frozen bunker chum can be purchased in plastic buckets with holes drilled in the buckets (or you may have to drill the holes), or in onion bags or some sort of mesh bags. Fluke are on the bottom, so that's where the chum needs to be. Do not tie the bucket or bag off a stern cleat so it floats right behind the boat. Depending on the strength of the current and the depth of the water, the chum may move well away from the boat before it ever gets anywhere near the

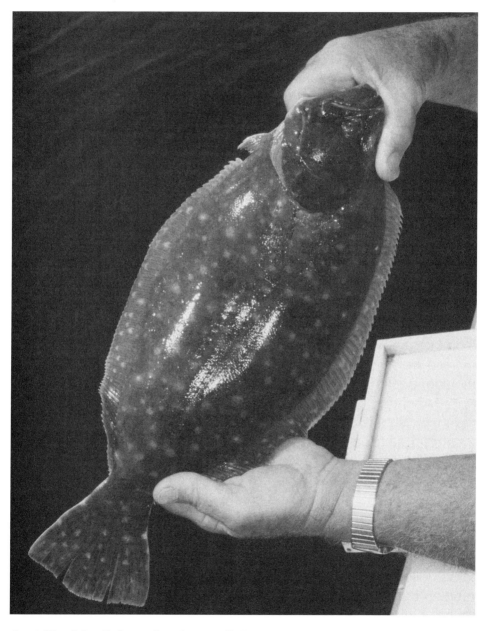

Just like bluefish and stripers, fluke will also move up a chum slick and devour the baits they encounter. When chumming for fluke, sink the chum container to the bottom.

bottom. Instead, sink the chum container to the bottom. Put a brick or heavy stone in with the chum in an onion bag or mesh bag and lower the bag on a rope to the bottom before tying it off on a cleat.

If the chum is in a plastic bucket, scoop some out and put it in a wire mesh chum pot and drop it to the bottom on a rope. Or weigh down the plastic bucket so it will sink. As the water melts the chum, small fish pieces and scent will seep through the holes in the bucket, or through the mesh in the bag or chum pot, and be carried along with the current.

Another way to get the chum deep can be borrowed from Alaskan halibut fisherman. Like us, these anglers are trying to attract flatfish to their boats via chum. In the strong currents they fish in, instead of weighting a chum bucket they simply tie it off to their anchor line, about five feet above the anchor, as it's lowered to the bottom. This not only gets the chum deep, it also places your baits far back in the chum slick, instead of right at the head of it. In a rip-roaring current, this tactic works well.

In shallow back bay areas, a smaller, do-it-yourself chum slick is often very effective. Slice into small pieces any leftover squid, clams, bunker, bluefish or croaker that may be available, and occasionally toss a few into the water. After the current has carried them well away from the boat, toss another handful.

Some anglers mix in rice, or dog food or cat food, to enhance their chum. Just be careful not to overdo it. The goal is to tempt fluke, to get them moving in search of a meal (your bait), and not to feed them with the chum.

Live baits such as snapper bluefish, spot, peanut bunker, small croaker and small white perch work very well in a chum slick. In fact, this is one situation in which live baits tend to out-fish strip baits. The anchored boat is not moving, so long strip baits may just hang on the hook or lay flat on the bottom instead of fluttering. Active live baits are sure to catch the eye of hungry fluke that are moving up through a chum slick. Fish live baits on a fish-finder rig or sliding egg sinker rig. In shallow-water back bay areas, it may be possible to fish live baits with only a split shot, or even no weight at all, as they will naturally swim toward the bottom. In this situation, remember that hooking the bait through the back, behind the dorsal fin, as opposed to lip-hooking it, will encourage it to swim downward.

Artificial lures can also be used to trigger strikes from fluke in a chum slick. A bucktail tipped with a strip bait, or a leadhead dressed with a plastic tail and/or strip bait, cast behind the boat and slowly retrieved along the bottom through the slick, will often get whacked. When chumming, I keep at the ready a spare spinning rod, with a small spoon or bucktail tied on. I'll occasionally cast it directly behind the boat, and let it sink way back in the chum slick, and then retrieve it quickly, with an erratic start-and-stop action, in hopes of hooking up with any small bluefish that may have invaded the slick. They are then used to provide an energetic live bait, or fresh strip baits, for fluke (as long as the bluefish meets any size limit that may be in place in the state I'm fishing in).

The time to anchor up for chumming is at the beginning of a tide, either incoming or outgoing. Current is needed to disburse chum, so don't waste fishing time by chumming during slack water periods. When there is no water movement the chum won't go any-where, or may just slowly sink to the bottom.

Make sure the container the chum is in (a mesh bag, mesh pot, plastic bucket) features small holes, so only small bits of chum can escape. If the chunks of chum are too big, fluke will be content to lay back and eat the chum; there will not be motivation for them to move up the slick in search of a meal.

Or, you can leave the drifting, trolling and anchoring to the pros. Party boat captains are on the water, weather permitting, prac-tically every day of the fluke season. They also are tied into a strong network of other party boat and charter boat captains whose liveli-hoods require them to find and catch fish for their customers. In ad-dition, party boat captains are very familiar with the structure and all of the fluke hot spots in their area.

PARTY BOAT FLUKING

One of the very biggest flounder I have even seen caught was hooked by an angler on a New Jersey party boat, and we weren't even flounder fishing! It was a nighttime bluefish trip. All of us along the rail had just hooked one or two dead butterfish through the eye sockets on an egg sinker rig and dropped it to the bottom. Before long, an angler cried out that he had one, and after a strong battle, we were all shocked when the big, brown flatfish appeared at the surface. The mate netted it and hoisted it aboard. The huge fluke was estimated to weigh about 14 pounds! The only flounder I have ever seen caught on a bluefish trip was one of the biggest flounder I have ever seen caught.

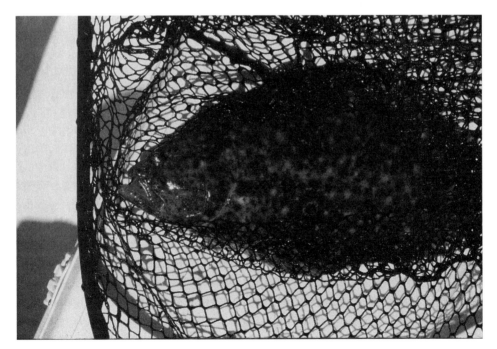

Thousands upon thousands of nice fluke are caught by anglers fishing from party boats each season.

There are hundreds of party boats, from New England to North Carolina, that run half-day, three-quarter-day, and full-day trips that specifically target flounder. Anglers haul tons of fluke up and over party boat rails each and every season. Party boats offer prime flounder fishing opportunities.

While rods, reels, rigs, sinkers and bait are usually available for daily rental on most head boats, it's recommended you take your own. You'll always be more comfortable and productive with the rods and reels you're familiar with. And on some boats, the gear they rent may be sub-par, or may have been damaged by a prior renter.

Most party boat sharpies fish with baitcasting or small conventional reels. They offer more line control, and with this type of fishing they're easier and more efficient than spinning reels. When the rig is dropped to the bottom, do not engage the spool, instead stop the line from coming off the spool by using your thumb to apply and maintain pressure on the spool. If contact with the bottom is lost, simply lift your thumb so line can come off the spool, getting the rig back down to the bottom. When a fluke pick-up is detected, lift your thumb to give the fluke just a little line before reeling in all slack and setting the hook.

Most fluke party boats provide every angler with a supply of squid strips. However, I also bring along a small cooler containing my own baits. A day or two before my party boat trip, I'll purchase squid at a local bait and tackle shop and cut it into long strips (the strips I cut for myself are usually considerably longer than what's provided on a party boat). I also bring along Fisherman's Choice and/or Pro Cut squid strips and squid worms. They're colored (red, yellow, green, white), scented (crab), pre-cut squid strips and squid worms. Of course, any sea robins, snapper bluefish, croaker or spot caught while flounder fishing on a party boat can be quickly cut into a supply of fresh strip baits.

Fluke rigs that are commonly used on party boats include homemade or store-bought top-bottom (high-low) rigs, and fish-finder rigs. If we're fishing depths of 25 feet or less and the current is not too strong, I sometimes like to fish with nothing more than a bucktail tied to the end of my line. I'll tip it with a strip bait, drop it to the bottom, and bounce it along by raising and lowering the rod tip. I'll frequently have to let out line to remain in contact with the bottom, yet bucktailing is a very productive fluke tactic, so it's well worth the effort.

No matter how you fish, bottom rig or bucktail, it's important that the sinker or bucktail weigh enough to maintain contact with the bottom, and that they're heavy enough to control so they don't snag other lines on the boat. I believe it's a good idea to use heavier sinkers and bucktails than you would on a private boat, to hopefully avoid hanging up with the increased lines in the water on a party boat trip. Plan to arrive at least 90 minutes to an hour before the head boat is scheduled to pull away from the dock. That will give you plenty of time to get your gear on board, and perhaps enjoy a cup of coffee before the trip gets underway. Plus, arriving early will give you a better opportunity to choose the fishing spot you want on the boat. Favored locations include the stern, especially the two corners, and up front in the bow. Fishing from the port or starboard side of a party boat can be productive as well, but you'll likely spend at least part of the day fishing under the boat, when you're on the down-current side and the captain sets up for a beam-to drift.

In addition to your favorite fluke fishing rod, reel, rigs and baits, other items you'll want to bring along include extra layers of warm and dry clothing, snacks and sandwiches and drinks on ice in a cooler separate from the bait, polarized sunglasses, knife and pliers, paper towels or a rag to wipe your hands, and plastic bags to take your fillets home in (if you will be cleaning your flounder at the party boat dock).

CHAPTER 8

TIPS AND TACTICS FROM EXPERTS

OUT OF THE ORR-DINARY

Andy Orr has caught flounder to nearly 10 pounds in Delaware Bay. One of the best days that Orr, his father and their fishing buddies have had (so far) produced a limit of 32 flounder, every single one of them was over 20 inches, and they were back at the dock before noon! Orr also makes and sells flounder rigs, umbrella rigs for striper trolling, and offshore trolling rigs. His nine pound, eight ounce doormat was caught on one of his rigs, and it was good for first place in the New Jersey Fluke Tournament that was held out of seven ports.

Orr is a terrific fisherman, and he uses innovative techniques to consistently catch big flounder. As this book was being written, Andy and I met for breakfast where he shared with me his flounder-catching tactics so they could be included. Here's what came out during our conversation.

His first rule is to fish his rigs as close to the boat as possible, even it means using heavier sinkers than most anglers are used to. Orr wants his rigs to sink straight down, or nearly straight down, and stay there. They should maintain contact with the bottom; it should not be necessary to occasionally let out more line to keep the sinker on the bottom. To accomplish this, Orr uses 10, 12, even 18 and 20 ounce sinkers, depending on the depth of the water and strength of the current. He recommends a flexible rod, and a baitcasting reel spooled with 50 pound test braided line.

Orr's convinced that rigs fished practically straight down from the boat provide the most natural presentation. If line is let out and the rig is fished farther from the boat, they'll either drag across the bottom or spin, and fluke won't be interested.

Big sinkers also provide another important benefit—they often initiate fluke strikes. Hefty sinkers thumping the bottom kick up puffs

Andy Orr uses big, heavy sinkers for fluke. He says they make it possible to fish rigs straight down from the boat, plus they thump bottom
and alert flounder that a bait is about to pass by.

of sand or mud, and also create vibrations and sounds that make fluke sit up and take notice. Then the fish will detect the pulse of the rig's spinning blade or spin-n-glow propeller, see the bucktail or plastic, and then the bait, prompting the flounder to lift off the bottom to attack.

Some days, Orr uses about one pound of weight specifically to pound the bottom. "Big fluke, you can't scare 'em," he says. Some flounder fishermen even like to tie a piece of chain to a length of rope and tie off the other end of the rope to a cleat in the boat. They toss over the chain so the drifting boat drags it across the bottom, creating a commotion that may trigger any flounder in the vicinity to feed. Orr typically fishes three rods at a time (or less, depending on what's legally allowed), all in rod holders, from the front of the boat (his father and fishing buddies get the middle and back of the boat). He uses heavy sinkers so his rigs bounce along the bottom, close to the boat. Ideally, he wants each sinker to hop about five yards at a time; in other words, there should be about five yards between one spot where the sinker hits bottom and the next spot. If the sinker's not hopping then it's dragging, and Orr will reel up and drop down again until the sinker bounces the way he wants it to.

He watches the rod tips carefully. The bending and straightening of the rod as the boat drifts will indicate if the sinker is bouncing along the bottom correctly, or if it's not and needs to reeled up and dropped down again. Also, with braided line, the vibrating rod tip will tell him that the spinner on the rig is working properly. If a rod tip suddenly moves differently, or stops moving like the other rods, a flounder has probably grabbed the bait.

The rod is pulled out of the rod holder, and Orr will take several steps back in the boat toward the fish, while lowering the rod tip toward the water, to provide a little additional line as the flounder continues to eat the bait. As the drifting boat pulls the line tight again, and he can feel the weight of the fluke on the line, Orr sets the hook hard and begins reeling. Even with braided line he sets the hook hard, saying it's necessary to drive the hook point into a flounder's hard, bony mouth. Do not pump a hooked flounder, instead, hold the rod steady and reel.

Concerning where to fish for flounder, Orr recommends the edges of shipping channels, humps, artificial reefs and other bottom structure; boils and eddies are often created on the surface over shoals and reefs as the current washes over and around the structure and these are areas he looks for when getting prepared to drop the lines.

On "hard" structure like reefs, wrecks, and rockpiles, Orr prefers to fish large, live bait such as croaker, spot and snapper bluefish. He'll use a palomar knot to tie a hook to the end of the leader. He leaves a long tag end, and ties a small treble hook to the tag end. The regular hook goes through the live bait's lips, nostrils or eye sockets, while one point of the treble hook is pierced through the bait's tail, providing a hook at both ends of the bait.

Orr and his father keep their boat at Money Island, New Jersey, and spend much of their season on Delaware Bay flounder fishing in the 25 to 32 foot depths at the Cross Ledge and near the Flat Top lighthouse (an old, abandoned lighthouse).

Orr also reminds us that flounder of the same size often hang out together in the same spot, so when a nice fish is caught, immediately toss over a buoy so you can return and fish that exact location again. Use the depthfinder and/or GPS to ensure that the next drift is the same as the previous drift, which produced the nice fish.

Dead tide is a very difficult time to effectively flounder fish. If a buoy had been deployed previously and several fish had been caught in that spot, return to it during dead tide and sit there, jigging up and down with a two-hook rig (high-low rig) baited with strip baits. The two strips darting up and down, and the sinker thumping the bottom, may be enough to attract nearby flounder to the rig. Another tactic while sitting still at dead tide is to fan cast with a bucktail baited with a strip bait. If a concentration of fish had not been located before the tide went slack, then bump the motor in and out of gear to generate boat movement in an attempt to find fish.

Even more discouraging than dead tide is the presence of sharks, stripers and porpoises. They eat flounder, and when they're around, flounder are more interested in hiding and staying alive than they are in eating.

The flounder rigs that Orr makes, sells and fishes with are used with a three-way swivel. The rigs feature a mono leader with a pre-tied loop on the end that makes it quick and easy to slip onto a the swivel eye. To the other end of the swivel, the angler ties on a short piece of mono with a loop tied in it to hold the sinker.

Leaders are monofilament or fluorocarbon of at least 40 pound test. On a typical day, Orr uses rigs with leaders that are 30 to 35 inches long from the three-way swivel to the hook. On calm days when the water is clear he'll use considerably longer leaders, sometimes up to 50 inches long. Frequently check the leader, and replace the rig if any nicks or abrasion are detected. Flounder are toothy fish, and one hooked fish can damage a rig.

Many of Orr's flounder rigs sport large, prominent plastic eyes, spinner blades, plastic beads and bucktail in white, green, pink and purple. He also ties flounder rigs featuring plastic squids. In 1997, Andy won the Junior National Fly Tying Championship—and that same commitment to quality materials and quality craftsmanship goes into each handmade rig.

One of his rigs features two squids rigged in tandem for extra flounder appeal. This rig is especially effectively in a very strong current, where the rig quickly moves along the bottom. The double squids make it easier for flounder to see and attack the rig as it darts by. Orr often uses 18 to 20 ounces of lead to hold this rig at or on bottom in a strong current. A strong current may make for difficult fishing conditions, but Orr says that's when some of the largest flounder are caught.

Orr never sends his rig to the bottom without checking it first. Before each and every drop, he lowers his rig just below the surface of the water, where he can see it and make sure the rig and bait are moving through the water naturally. If the blade isn't spinning freely, if the bucktail or plastic doesn't look neat and natural, or if the rig spins even slightly, he'll lift it back in the boat for some fine-tuning. If that doesn't correct the problem, the rig is replaced with a new one. He constantly checks the hook to make sure it's sharp and there's absolutely nothing on the point of the hook. One teeny, tiny scale from a previously-caught flounder may prevent the hook from penetrating the mouth of the next fish that bites.

Orr's fierce attention to detail is a characteristic shared by many of the expert fluke fishermen that I have had the privilege to fish with over the years. On the water, they're constantly focused on catching flounder. They keep a close eye on everything that's going on. They leave nothing to chance –anything that doesn't appear just right is immediately corrected or replaced. Nothing less than perfection is acceptable.

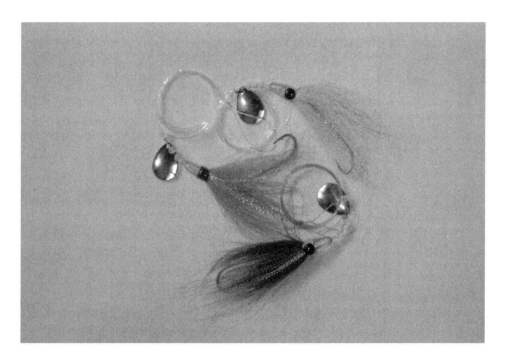

Enticing flounder rigs, created by Andy Orr at AMO Tackle.

Once, during a visit to Ocean City Inlet in Maryland, Orr watched as a 15 year-old angler he did not know caught two 20 inch flounder. But then the young fisherman ran out of bait. Orr offered to help, and tied one of his handmade flounder rigs on the boy's line, and baited it with a whole squid and a big killie that Orr had. Following Orr's recommendation, the youngster dropped the rig in an eddy that had formed near the inlet rocks. Suddenly, the youngster set the hook, battled a strong, determined fish, and dragged a huge 30-inch, nine pound flounder out of the inlet!

Orr's rigs are available in several Mid Atlantic tackle shops; as his business grows, expect them to start showing up in other bait and tackle shops in Maryland, Delaware, Virginia, Pennsylvania and beyond. For more information about his rigs, call (717) 823-3120, or email amo.fish@hotmail.com.

BOB'S SCHOOL OF BOAT CONTROL

When you walk into Bob Baker's home in southern Delaware, you're greeted by numerous buck mounts on every wall in the living room. Big, beautiful, trophy eight pointers and better. Not all are Bob's, as several of the nice whitetail deer, including the biggest buck of them all, was shot by his wife Lee. The Bakers have shot more than 100 buck in Delaware, Maryland, Alabama, Texas and Canada. But there's more than hunting trophies on the wall—also prominently displayed is a replica of the magnificent 11 pound, two ounce, 30-inch doormat flounder Bob Baker nailed in the Lewes/Rehoboth Canal in Lewes, Delaware on June 10, 2006.

Every bedroom is tastefully decorated with more mounts, including deer, big chain pickerel, and a stringer of lunker largemouth bass over seven pounds. It's obvious that Bob Baker is an avid outdoorsman, and a very successful hunter and fisherman. He possesses a thorough understanding of the characteristics, habits and movements of the game and fish that he pursues. I flounder fished with Baker at Wachapreague, Virginia, so I could see how he does it, pick his brain for tips and tactics, and share his expertise with readers of this book.

Twenty-five years ago, when the plant he was working for closed, Bob became a freshwater fishing guide on southern Delaware ponds to support his family. When a friend took him flounder fishing at Wachapreague, Baker enjoyed it tremendously, and soon became a flounder guide in Virginia, fishing in Wachapreague, Chincoteague, Quinby, and Folly's Creek. His livelihood depended on his ability to locate and catch flounder for his clients, so he had to learn quickly—and he did. While he is now retired from guiding, he still makes about 50 trips a year to Virginia, plus trips to Delaware and

Bob Baker nailed this trophy 11 pound, two ounce flounder in Delaware in June of 2006.

Chesapeake bays, for his flounder fishing enjoyment. He's accumulated a lot of flounder know-how during the more than 1,200 flounder trips he has made during the past two-and-a-half decades.

Priority one in Baker's opinion is proper boat positioning to keep the baits in the strike zone, and he works hard at it. Keeping the boat over productive bottom is especially challenging in locations like Wachapreague, which feature channels, guts and marshes (there are many back bay and interior coastal water areas like this in states up and down the East Coast). The channels, guts and marshes curve and snake around; there are very few prolonged straight-away drifting opportunities.

"Take what the sea and wind give you," Baker says. He frequently checks the weather and wind forecast in the days and hours leading up to his trip. He is also aware of the tides for the day. Upon arrival at the dock, he carefully checks the wind direction and speed, and this allows him to rule out specific locations where the wind will be against the tide. (These locations will change during the day as the tide and/or wind direction change, so keep a close eye on wind speed and direction all day long.)

Since the narrow channels curve through the marshes, there will be few locations where conditions will be most favorable, with the breeze blowing in the same direction as the tide. Instead, most areas will have the wind blowing across the channel. The most productive fishing comes while drifting straight in the channel, not while being blown by the wind across the current, and across the channel. A breeze blowing across the channel results in unproductive fishing; however, Baker takes a very hands-on approach to overcome it.

He keeps the motor on his Quintrex 162 center console running all day long. When he sets up for a drift, he makes sure the stern of the boat is facing into the wind. Baited rigs are lowered to the bottom and rods placed in rod holders on the side of the boat where the rigs won't go under the boat. While the boat drifts with the current it will begin to move across the channel because of the wind. But before it gets very far, Baker nudges the motor into reverse to slowly move the boat back in the channel, then the motor is put in neutral

Bob Baker drifts with his stern to the wind, and frequently bumps his motor into gear to offset the affects of the wind. He works to maintain proper boat positioning and to keep baits in the strike zone.

again.

Then, before long, Baker backs up again to make up for the positioning that was lost to the wind. This process, this zigzag back-and-forth pattern as the boat drifts with the current, is repeated over and over again on each drift. Depending on the strength of the wind, Baker may have to re-position the boat every 60 seconds, or even more frequently than that. He does whatever it takes to keep the boat drifting with the current in the channel so the baits remain over the most productive bottom.

Allowing the boat to drift across the channel is unproductive and a waste of fishing time. When this is allowed to occur, the boat moves quickly across and out of the channel; rigs and baits spend very little time in the productive zone, and too much time out of the channel and in areas where there are no fish. Plus, rigs and baits moving across the current provide an unnatural appearance as compared to rigs and baits that are maintained in the channel where they drift with the current.

According to Baker, it is easier to control and re-position a boat with the stern into the breeze, rather than the bow. A breeze blowing against the bow tends to push the bow and turn the boat one direction or another, which messes up the drift. However, the wind against the wide, flat stern pushes the boat straight, and the boat can be brought back with a quick nudge into reverse and backing straight down. Baker says it also takes more gas, and the boat moves too quickly, when it's moved and repositioned in forward.

Baker was using this proactive approach to drifting when he nailed his doormat 11 pound, two ounce flounder in the Lewes/Rehoboth Canal. This drifting technique will work in canals, channels and guts from New England to North Carolina.

Baker fishes two or three (or whatever amount is legal) rods in rod holders. This keeps his hands free to re-position the boat. All of his spinning rods and reels are the same, so he's very familiar with the action of the rods. He keeps a close and constant eye on his rod tips, and he can immediately detect any type of unusual, subtle movement in the tip, which indicates a bite. If the rod bends

Adjustable rod holders make it possible to fish several rods at a time while keeping hands free for boat positioning.

more than normal, even slightly, this means a flounder has probably grabbed the bait, and the rod tip is lowered to provide line for the fish to begin swallowing the bait. A moment later, the hook is set. Instead of bending, if the rod tip is bouncing, Baker will immediately set the hook.

Wachapreague is famous for its fantastic early-spring flounder action (usually during the months of April and May), and anglers from Virginia, North Carolina, Maryland, Delaware, Pennsylvania and beyond trailer their boats to the Eastern Shore to kick-off their season in Wachapreague. Generally speaking, in the early season when air and water temperatures can still be downright chilly, an outgoing tide will be most productive, especially in the afternoon on a clear day when water at high tide has been warmed by the sun.

In early April, most flounder are caught in the deeper channels and holes. By the end of April and into May, they'll move up and can be caught in the shallows and on the shallow flats. The last two hours of an outgoing tide will usually concentrate flounder in the deeper channels and holes, while the best tide for fishing the shallows is the last two hours of an incoming tide, when there is the most water in the shallows and on the flats. The beginning of an outgoing tide can also be quite productive, as it will pull baitfish from the shallows and put flounder on the feed.

Baker said many anglers are unaware of the outstanding summertime and fall flounder fishing opportunities at Wachapreague. In June and July, plenty of nice flounder can be caught, especially in deeper water near the inlet. An incoming tide bringing in cooler water from the ocean will usually trigger the best bite. In the fall when the water begins to cool, flounder can be caught in the shallow water once again.

In locations like Wachapreague, with channels, guts and backbay marshes, Baker recommends spending time at dead low tide moving around and looking around. Check out bottom contours and structure that may be visible at low tide. Learn which shallow-water areas and flats drain at low tide, and which will still hold enough water for fishing (remember, wind speed and direction, and also moon phases, will have a significant affect). Dead low tide is a great time to explore and learn more about how and where to fish.

In the winter, Baker spends a lot of time at his home work-bench tying up the bucktails, fluke killers and other items he uses to construct his high/low flounder rigs. A swivel is tied to one end of a three to four foot long piece of 40 pound mono or fluorocarbon leader (for connecting the rig to the line from the reel), and a snap swivel is tied to the other end (the bottom end, for holding the sinker). Two dropper loops are tied in the leader. A fluke killer (green or chartreuse bucktail skirt with beads and a spinnerblade) on an 18 inch leader goes on the bottom loop, while a small bucktail gets slipped on the top loop.

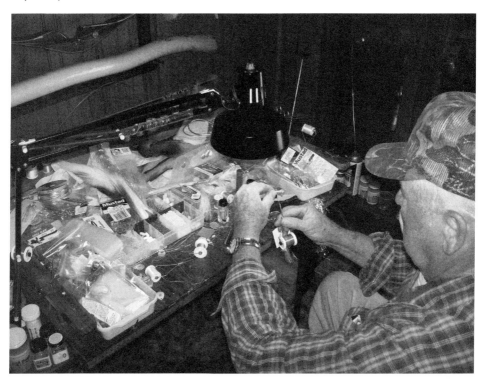

Use your knowledge of fluke and their feeding habits, your fishing ex-periences, and your creativity to create bottom rigs that are perfectly suited for your fluke fishing needs.

Baker hooks one or two frozen silversides through the eyes on the bucktail. The fluke killer gets baited with a squid strip and a bull minnow, or a strip of cut bait. Baker says the bucktail with silversides on the top loop catches 60 percent of his flounder, including most of the bigger fish.

His favorite bucktail colors include an orange head with pearl Flashabou, or an orange head with chartreuse Flashabou or deer hair. Those colors work well in most water conditions. In dingy water, Baker favors a yellow or chartreuse bucktail, while all-white bucktails seem to catch more of the fish in clear-water conditions.

At Wachapreague, Delaware Bay, Chesapeake Bay or anywhere there are flounder, to specifically target the biggest flatties, fish "on structure in deep water." Baker recommends the periods of slower current, such as the very end or very beginning of an incoming or outgoing tide. It's easier to fish deeper water with a natural presentation in a slower current.

During the past quarter century, Bob Baker has made about 50 trips a year to Wachapreague. That's more than 1,200 trips in all! He's been "skunked" only six or seven times. He hasn't always caught big fish, and he hasn't always caught lots of flounder, but he has used his skills and experience to consistently locate and catch at least a few flounder. I appreciate the information and techniques he has shared with us!

CASTING AND FLOAT FISHING LESSONS FROM PETE

"I always have more than one club in my bag," is how long-time flounder fisherman Pete Dressler compares his fluke fishing preparedness to golf. When his Grady White rolls off the trailer to fish Chesapeake Bay, Delaware Bay or other fluke locations, Dressler is always geared up and ready to drift, to troll, to anchor, even to fish bait under a float. It all depends on which approach will be most productive depending on the tide, wind, the fish and other factors.

Dressler views a fishing trip as a "return on investment, and the investment is time." His goal is to cover the most productive bottom, and catch the most fish, in the shortest amount of time. And he's an expert at it! I have fished with Dressler several times, enjoyed myself tremendously, and saw firsthand just how productive his techniques are.

When a fish is hooked, Dressler will quickly re-position the boat for another drift over the same location. If another fish is hooked there, Dressler will toss over a marker jug. Flounder will bunch up together in a relatively small spot on a piece of structure. The hot spot, or "area of opportunity" as Dressler calls it, may be only 10 yards wide, such as when flounder are positioned on a narrow edge facing into the current. When drifting or trolling, baits will quickly move through the hot spot, resulting in lots of unproductive fishing time when the baits are not in the fish.

To make the best use of his fishing time, and to keep his bait among the flounder for as long as possible, Dressler will anchor and cast around his marker jug, especially in shallow-water locations. When casting for fluke, Dressler uses a six foot to six and a half foot rod, and a spinning reel spooled with 10 pound test braided line. The key advantage of braided line in this situation is its super sensitivity, making it possible to easily detect the motion and action of the bait, its contact with the bottom, and flounder strikes.

A 25 to 40 pound mono leader (24 to 36 inches long) is attached to the braided line via a small swivel. Dressler says flounder are not leader shy, so he uses heavy, stiff leader material because it does not tangle.

A leadhead jig, heavy enough to cut through the current and reach bottom, preferably with a 1/0 long-shank thin-wire hook, is tied to the end of the leader. A long-shank hook is easier and safer to grab and hold when unhooking toothy fluke. It's baited with a strip bait, or a big bull minnow (a minnow moves more naturally on a thin-wire hook).

Dressler casts and works the jighead and bait across the current, or casts up-current and jigs it back to the boat with the current. It's important to cast accurately so that each retrieve brings the leadhead over the exact spot where the previous fish were caught.

Twitching the rod tip will bounce and skip the leadhead, and flutter the strip bait or swim the minnow along the bottom. When a strike, or extra weight, is detected, Dressler immediately sets the hook. With an immediate hookset, undersized fish will not be hooked deeply.

Anchoring makes it possible to concentrate casts, and present baits, right where the fish are. Casting jigheads is especially effective in canals, channels and on shallow flats at high tide when flounder move in to feast on mantis shrimp and baitfish.

Casting with jigheads works well on sandy and mud bottom areas. However, in locations where there is vegetation on the bottom, the jighead will foul weeds, and also discolor the strip bait. Flounder will lurk in weeds, and a great way to catch fluke in the grass is to

Cast and work the jighead and bait across the current, or cast up-current and jigs it back to the boat with the current.

present a bait just above the vegetation with a float rig.

Dressler uses a large float in which the leader is fed through the float, and the float is stopped on the leader with a bead. After being fed through the float, the end of the leader is tied to a three-quarter ounce or one ounce cigar sinker. A length of leader is tied to the other (bottom) ring on the sinker, and a hook is tied to the other end of the leader. (The float must be big enough to float with a one ounce sinker tied below it.)

The lengths of the leaders from the float to the sinker, and from the sinker to the hook, are determined by the distance between

Don't be sinker shy. Heavy sinkers are often needed for effective trolling and drifting.

the surface of the water and the top of the vegetation. A big bull min-now hooked through the lips on a thin-wire hook should swim just above the top of the grass. Fish from an anchored boat, allowing the current to push the float rig away from the boat and over the vegetation.

During an incoming tide, fluke will follow bait right up into shal-low-water locations, and Dressler will locate and catch flounder by trolling in the shallows (make sure the water is deep enough for safe trolling, and keep an eye out for rocks, stumps and other obstruc-tions on the bottom that could damage the boat or lower unit).

Dressler's boat and kicker motor enable him to troll in water as shallow as two feet. He uses heavy sinkers to keep the rig prac-tically straight down from the moving boat; he has caught flounder while trolling in 24 inches of water, with 10 ounce sinkers and the rig right behind the boat, in the prop wash! Dressler says he can usu-ally see the strip bait in the wash, and suddenly, it will no longer be visible—that means a fluke has grabbed it! At times, Dressler said he has seen flounder (it appears as a dark spot in the water behind the boat), swimming with the bait it has grabbed as the bait is pulled along by the trolling boat.

When trolling 20 to 80 foot depths with eight to 20 ounce sink-ers, Dressler beefs up his tackle to a six foot heavy-action long-han-dled rod, and a conventional levelwind reel with a big, easy-to-use handle, and a durable drag. The reel is spooled with 20 to 40 pound braided line. Rods are placed in rod holders and a close eye is kept on the rod tips.

On boats with motors of any size, Dressler says the motor usually moves the boat too fast while trolling, even when it's bumped down to practically neutral. To prevent this, he installed a nine point nine horsepower kicker motor on the transom of his Grady White. It features an extended handle so it can be steered without the need to stand right by the motor. Also mounted in the stern of the boat is a second depthfinder, so Dressler can easily read it while operating the kicker motor—he makes sure he is using the kicker to maintain his trolling pattern directly over productive bottom structure.

Dressler has his kicker motor rigged totally separate from the big motor. The kicker features an electric start, and a pull start. That way, if there's a problem with the big motor, or contaminated gas, or an electrical problem, the kicker also serves as an important safety feature and can be used to get Dressler home.

Pete Dressler is prepared for productive flounder fishing. Note the Suzuki kicker motor with extended handle for trolling, and the stern-mounted depthfinder to the left of the black Mercury motor.

A few final, general tips passed along by Dressler: he likes to always be using leaders that are about three feet long; any longer than that and they may drag on the bottom, possibly chaffing or snagging. When cutting bait strips from sea robins, don't hesitate to use strips with the darker skin and scales from high on the sea robin's back. Dressler feels they're just as effective as white belly strips taken from the same fish. And finally, Dressler lets us in on his favorite bottom rig: one featuring a chartreuse or green plastic squid skirt is the top pick.

Dressler uses a baitcasting reel (top) for shallow-water trolling, and a conventional levelwind reel (bottom) when trolling with heaver sinkers in deeper water.

CHAPTER 9

ONCE YOU'VE HOOKED 'EM

It's the ultimate moment in fishing—we get a bite, set the hook and fight a fish! This is what we plan for, prepare for and hope for. Many of us put a lot of time, effort and money into fishing, and battling a big fish on the end of the line is what it's all about.

It begins with a bite. Next comes the drop-back. Then the tight line, and the bent rod. Fighting a fish is the most exciting and enjoyable moment in the sport. Before it occurs, it's important to properly set the drag. While fluke aren't the most ferocious fighters in the ocean, they are no slouches, either. They make good use of their

It all begins with a bite...when the weight of the fish is detected, the hook is set.

broad bodies, dogged determination and strength in attempts to free themselves from the hook. Big fluke are especially challenging adversaries, famous for their violent head shakes.

DRAG DONE RIGHT

If your drag isn't set properly, there's a good chance your line will snap and your next meal will swim away. A general rule is that the drag should be set at about 25 percent of the line's pound test rating. With 12 pound test line, the drag should give line when about three pounds of pressure is applied. With 17 pound test, the drag should be set at about four and a quarter pounds of pressure. For 20 pound line, use a drag setting of about five pounds. To most accurately set a drag, tie the end of the line to a hand scale and pull the hand scale until line comes off the reel. The scale will indicate how many pounds of pressure are being applied when the drag starts to give line, and the drag can be set accordingly.

Most fishermen, myself included, most often set drags by feel. We grab the line in front of the reel and pull, and tighten or loosen the drag until it gives line at what seems like a reasonable amount of pressure. But be careful. When a drag is set like this, it's almost always exceeds 25 percent of the line's pound test rating. This isn't a problem with most of the fluke we catch; however, it could be costly at the most inopportune of times. When a big barn-door fluke is brought to boatside, and there's little line between the rod tip and the fish, the line (especially with monofilament, which usually has some extra give thanks to its stretching properties when a lot of line is out) may break if the big fish makes a sudden and strong surge and the drag is set too tightly.

FIGHTING FLUKE

When battling hooked fluke, hold the rod steady and reel. Do not pump the rod, because raising the rod tip, and then reeling in slack as the rod tip is lowered, may for an instant create slack in the line—which is all that is needed for a fish to come free of the hook. Hold the rod so the fish is fighting the rod; do not point the rod at the water or fish, which takes the bend in the rod out of the fish-fighting equasion. The flex of the rod keeps constant pressure on the fish, and holds the hook tight in its mouth. The rod will absorb much of the shock and pressure that are applied when a strong fish dives for the bottom or violently shakes it head.

Do not raise and lower the rod tip when fighting hooked fluke. Instead, hold the rod steady and reel. Always keep the line tight.

If a trophy fluke is hooked and pulls so hard the drag gives line, avoid the temptation to press down with your thumb on the spool of a baitcasting or conventional reel, or to press against the edge of the spool on a spinning reel. This is commonly called "thumbing" the drag, and the sudden stop may result in the fluke of a lifetime being lost to a broken line. The drag is an important feature and you need to allow it to do its job. Also remember that with a spinning reel, do not try to reel in line as line is being pulled from the drag, as this will result in line twist.

For flounder, use long-handled nets with wide openings so the fish can be easily slipped into the hoop. As a fish is worked close to the boat, the amount of line between the rod tip and the fish diminishes, resulting in no more stretching or cushioning provided by monofilament. Any mistake the angler makes now will be magnified, so stay alert and focused. Until the fluke actually hits the deck of the boat, things can still go wrong. Be prepared to react quickly, as flounder often make a quick dash under the boat, once they see it. It may be necessary to lower the rod tip, or even stick the rod tip in the water, to help prevent line from being rubbed against the boat or tangled in the prop.

INTO THE NET

When a fluke seems under control at boatside do not lift its head from the water, or the fish may be lost. Always remember that as long as the fish is in the water, part of its weight is supported by the water. Lift its head clear of the surface, and you are magnifying the amount of pressure on the line at that moment. Keep the line constantly taut. Make sure the net is untangled and well clear of cleats and other items on the boat that the net could catch on. Always net fluke (and other fish, for that matter) head first. Dipping the net behind a fluke may cause it to bolt forward, away from the net. Fish don't swim in reverse, so they won't swim into a net behind them, and you don't want to be "chasing" them through the water with the net. Put the net in the water ahead of the fluke and net it headfirst.

Obviously, all fluke we catch will not be not large enough to keep. We must release all undersized fish, and we want them to survive. Net and handle them with care. Frabill and other companies offer knotless nets, nets that have been specially treated so as not to damage the scales or rub off a fish's protective slime. If possible, it's best to remove the hook from clearly undersized fish while they are still in the water. If you must bring one into the boat to remove the hook, handle it with a wet rag in your hands. (It's important to wet the rag first, or it will remove some of the fish's protective layer of slime, possibly causing infection.) Carefully and gently remove hooks from undersized fish. A pair of long needle-nose pliers, or any one of a number of de-hooker devices, can be used to unhook fluke, even fish with the hook deep in its throat. Once the hook is free, slide the fish gently back into the water, head-first. Never throw or toss the fish away from the boat, because it can send the fish into shock.

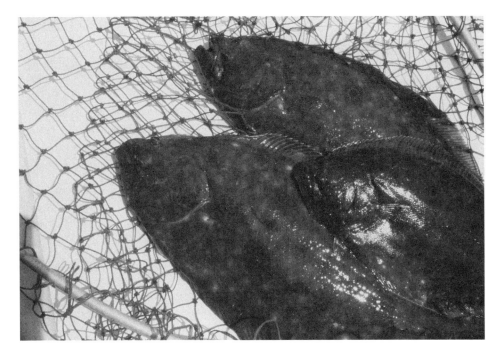

Always net flounder head first.

CHAPTER 10

TOP EAST COAST FLOUNDER HOTSPOTS

From skinny water less than 12 inches deep, to depths of 100 feet or more. From guts, tidal creeks, piers, docks and bridges, on out to the open ocean. Fluke are caught in many, many near-shore locations and on the inshore grounds. One of the most appealing aspects of fluke is their widespread availability. These fish are caught in hundreds of thousands of locations each season from New England to Florida. There are so many good spots that it's impossible to list them all in a single book. This chapter will, however, pinpoint a few popular and productive locations that consistently provide excellent fluke fishing season after season, and should be ranked high on your list of "must-fish" fluke fishing destinations.

In addition to fishing the proven locations, there's also a great deal of personal satisfaction that comes from using your fishing experience, and your understanding of fluke and their feeding habits, to discover your own fluke fishing hot spots. Experiment, identify and fish locations and bottom structure you believe should hold fluke, make each day on the water a learning experience, have fun while doing it, and good luck!

Before jumping right into these hotspots: one must realize that from season to season, and even from week to week, hotspots will come and go. You may load the boat in a specific spot one day, then return the next to find it barren. You can't expect to catch quality fish in any specific place, simply because it is known as a "good spot." There are, however, certain areas up and down the coast that offer reliably good fishing year after year. For anglers that enjoy traveling to new waters, or are maybe just looking for a new hotspot close to home, they are included here.

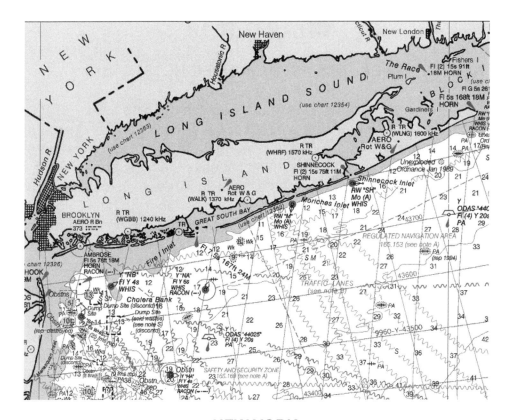

NEW YORK

Fluke are extremely popular in New York waters, but don't dare call them "flounder" up here or the locals won't even know what fish you're talking about. Although the season is slightly shorter this far north than it is for most other flounder territories, New Yorkers are treated to the ability to target extremely large fluke.

The first place this is true of is at the very tip of Long Island, near Montauk, New York. Rich in fishing history, this area is also rich in flatfish. Look at the first New York chart, and you'll see that the first New York hotspot, NY #1, is not a single spot so much as a broad swath of beach from the Montauk Rips down to Shinnecock Inlet. Fluke can be caught in this area throughout the season, especially by drifting baits through the rips, at the drop-off just off the beach, and near the inlet. What really makes this spot important, however, is the fact that flatfish migrating out of Long Island Sound, the Rips, and surrounding areas all turn right after they pass the last bit of land, and follow this edge south to begin their fall journey to warmer waters. Anglers in the know will drift live baits—live snapper blues and spearing are considered top choices—along this edge, starting in the month of September and often running through the month of October, to catch these fish. Unusually large flounder in the double-digit class are about as common here, at this time, as they are anywhere else along the entire east coast, at any given time. So, if you want to target trophy fluke, this is as good place and time as any other to do it.

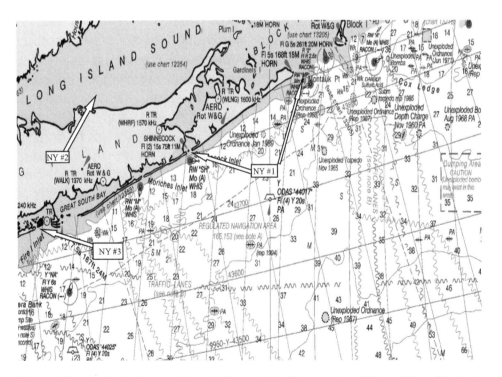

From Montauk to Long Island Sound to Hempstead Bay, New York is chock full of prime fluke territory.

The whole of Long Island Sound, marked as NY #2 on this chart, holds good fluke fishing through the summer and into the fall. Most anglers will drift the channel edges here, using the old stand-by minnow/squid sandwich baits dragged on some sort of fluke killer or top/bottom rig.

Long Island Sound is a big body of water, but there are a few specific areas to take note of. One area that sees nice summer runs of fluke more years than not is the series of drop-offs on the south side of Fischer Island, in the north-eastern end of the sound. Gardiners Bay, also in the eastern sound, is another common fluke hotspot. The mouths of the Mystic, Niantic, and Connecticut Rivers are also good areas to hunt down flatfish during the warm months of the year, and into the fall.

Don't think for a minute that you can't catch flounder farther to the south, however. Fire Island Inlet, marked by NY #3, is another area that sees a strong run of flounder every year. And since this inlet leads directly to the ocean, it sees a stronger, more concentrated spring run of fish than the sound does. In the bay behind the inlet, Great South Bay, it is mostly open water and as in Long island sound, most of the flounder sharpies in this area will stick to drifting channel edges with baited fluke killer rigs. This changes, however, as you head down into Hempstead Bay. Here, the waters consist of channels, cuts, and sloughs running through marsh islands. Fishing tactics change accordingly. Many anglers still drift with bait, but here it's also popular to cast and retrieve with bucktails tipped with squid strips or minnow, or leadhead jigs with plastic tails. Areas like Garrett Lead, Hog Island Channel, and Shell Creek are all full of fish. Focusing in on fluke, however, one should look specifically for the cuts in this area that have deep channels with shallow shelves on one side or the other (Broad Channel, behind Long Beach is one good example.) At high tide you can cast and retrieve on those shelves to catch the fluke, and as the tide drops, shift to drifting along the deeper channel edges.

Closer to the largest city in the nation, in the waters near the mouth of the Hudson, there is surprisingly good fluke fishing. Currents here are strong, and although one might think close proximity to New York City would ruin the fishing, it just isn't so. In fact, the drop-offs along both the eastern and western edges of the channel, near the NY #4 area, hold plenty of fluke from mid to late May through October. This is fairly deep water, so most fluke fishing takes place here with heavy gear and plenty of weight, often rigged up with braid or wire line if you intend to troll.

The drop-offs on the east side of Coney Island should also be checked out with a minnow-squid combination, as should the drops on the south side of Staten Island. Farther out into the New York entrance and Lower Bay, in the area marked by NY #5, the two main shipping channels (Ambrose and Chapel Hill) are usually targeted by

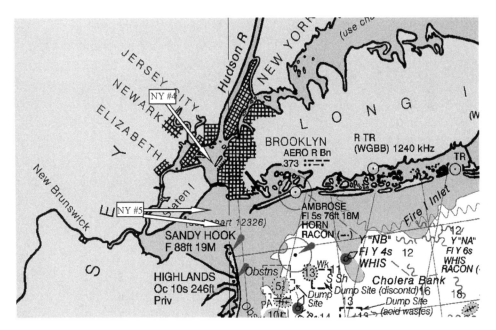

This area may be crowded with people, but there's also a crowd of fluke near by.

anglers looking for bluefish, stripers, and weakfish. But in-between the two channels, near where they meet, Roamer Shoal rises up out of the depths and provides good structure for fluke. As you might expect, look to find the fluke up on the edges of the shoals during high tides, and hunt for them closer to the drop-offs and channel edges when the tide is low and/or running out.

NEW JERSEY

New Jersey has a long, proud history of fishing, and as with New York, it's surprising how much excellent angling is waiting for you so close to major metropolitan areas. Much of Jersey's fluke waters consists of coastal bays and near-shore reefs, plus parts of the mouth of the Delaware Bay. Form north to south, here's where you'll want to go one the hunt, for fluke.

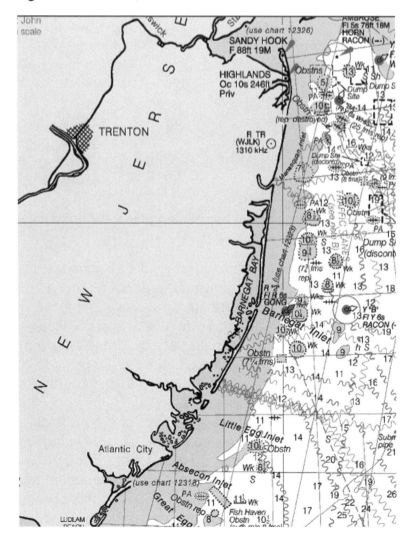

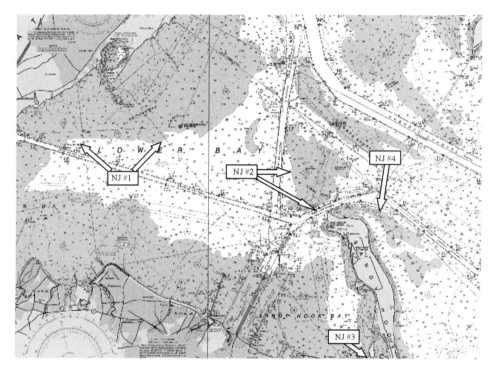

The state of New Jersey is a happening place, for fluke anglers.

The first area of interest to Jersey fluke aficionados, NJ #1, is the area full of shoal edges in Lower Bay. Although this area is better known for winter flounder, the fluke's cousin, and these fish are found on the flat, muddy bottom in relatively shallow water, conditions are better for summer flounder very close by. Where the flats drop off into deeper water is the place that fluke are going to become the dominant species. Drifting these edges with minnow and/or squid on fluke killers is the norm in these waters.

A bit farther east there are a number of drop-offs on the numerous shipping channel edges, found at NJ #2. During outgoing tide in particular, fluke will gather up along these edges and fall for fluke killers, or spearing or strip baits fished on top/bottom rigs. This area is frequented by party boats, which often fish this zone for both fluke and in the deeper channel areas for weakfish. If you want to try fishing here and don't have a boat, you can still head for Sandy Hook. Several party boats like the Atlantic Star fish for half or full days, (the Atlantic Star, http://mysite.verizon.net/atlantic_star/index. htm, is $35 for adults and $23 for kids, for half-day trips) and they specialize in putting you on the fluke. The Elaine B II is another boat that works these waters (732/541-2169 or www.elaineb2.com) and it does three-quarter days focusing on fluke, as well as making trips for other species for both full and half days.

Up behind Sandy Hook, at NJ #3, you'll find holes and shoals near the mouth of the Shrewsbury River, which are in protected water. This is a great area to head for when the winds are out of the south or east, and make open water too uncomfortable for fishing. Try jigging bucktails tipped with squid strips in the holes during ebb tides, and on full tides, cast and retrieve the bucktail along the edges of the holes and up into the shallow water surrounding them.

NJ #4 marks the king of all the hotspots in this area, the rips at Sandy Hook. This area is better known for its striper and bluefish fisheries, but like many hotspots known for different species, if you fish on the bottom here, you'll find big flounder on the prowl. This is a high-current area and is often rough, so heavy weights and gear are the norm. Wire-line and/or braid trolling is particularly effective in these conditions.

The Shark River inlet, marked by NJ #6, is a relatively tight, high-current area. Naturally, this attracts fish that are on the feed, including fluke. Fishing around the channel edges will produce fish, but once summer sets in the fishing is quite often better just outside the inlet, among the shoal edges to the north and south of the channel, then it is inside the inlet itself. One exception to this is at the NJ #7 spot, where the channel edges meet muddy shoals and flats. During low tides much of the mud flats will be exposed. Early in the season, when water temperatures are just within the flounder's preferred range, you can use these flats to your advantage: plan on arriving here at about mid-tide, as the water is incoming, on a bright, sunny day. When the flats are exposed they're warmed by the sun. Then, when the water comes up and covers them, these become hotspots—quite literally. The mud will retain some of the heat from the sun, and fish will move up from the channel edges to enjoy the warmth as they hunt. Position your boat so it's right on the edge of the channel, and cast bucktails trimmed with squid strips, or plastic tails on jigheads, up into the shallower water. Then bounce your offering along the bottom as you retrieve it.

At Manasquan Inlet, again, you'll find fairly fast moving water and some muddy flats that link up with channel edges. Apply similar techniques here. Pay special attention to the point marked by NJ #8. The four to six foot deep shoal, with a deep channel on one side and shallow flats on the other, is a good area for both casting lures and for drifting minnow or minnow/squid combination baits on fluke killers

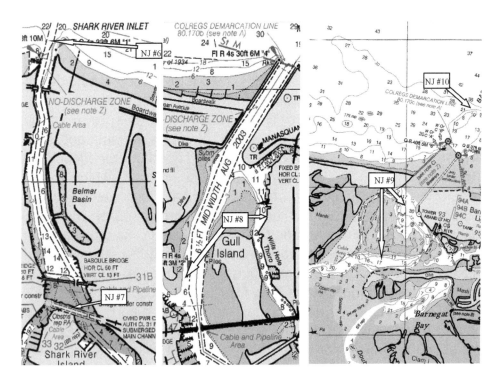

Jersey's coastline offers inlets, bays, and near-shore reefs and wrecks—and all hold fluke.

or top/bottom rigs.

Down at Barnegat Bay you'll find less restricted deepwater areas, as well as nice shoals and drops both inside and outside of the inlet. In the protected waters just inside of the inlet, there's excellent fishing around the sandy shoal edges, usually through the entire season. On the outside, pay particular attention to the shoal marked by NJ #10. Try drifting from deep water up the edge, onto the shoal, then back into the deep water. Remember to be careful to mark the exact depth in which you get bites, as the fluke will orient to a specific depth range during each particular cycle of the tide. On high tides expect them to be found shallower on the shoal, and on low tides, look for them to pop up on the edges and in the deeper water. This spot can get particularly hot in the early fall, as mullet migrate out into the open ocean and down the coast. During this time frame, you may want to try to fish with live finger mullet in the four to six inch size range (match the hatch!) if they are attainable.

Moving into Barnegat Bay itself, look for the holes and deep-water edges marked by NJ hotspot #11. Any of the edges in this vicinity are a good bet, once flounder have moved through the inlet in the spring months. The hole right near the bridge (marked by the shortest arrow at this hot spot) is a good area to jig for the flatties, as there's deep water on the south side of Pelican Island which sometimes concentrates the fish. So far as the mid-bay channels go, drifting or slowly trolling through these areas is usually the best call, as the fish will tend to be scattered along the edges over long distances. This is also true at the channel marked by NJ #12. Plan to fish here later in the season, once the waters have warmed thoroughly and the fish have spread out throughout the bay.

At Oyster Creek channel, marked on the lower chart continu-ing Barnegat Bay, by NJ #13, there are more deep water cuts with shallow sandy bars around the edges. This is a good area to hit early in the season before the fish have all moved through the inlet and scattered, and remains a good spot to try through the season.

If you have a boat that can handle leaving the inlet in your wake, during the summertime often your best bet for catching larger class fish will come by fishing the near-shore wrecks and reefs. You'll find one of these at the spot marked by NJ #14. This is the Sandy Hook reef site. The water here is 45 to 55 feet deep, and many kinds of materials were planted here years ago to attract bottom fish. Go to coordinates 40'22.14 x 73'56.23, drop a marker buoy, and run your

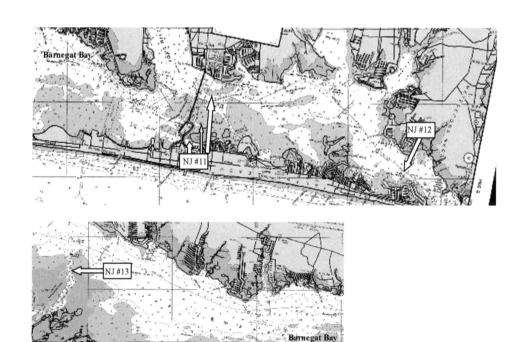

Inside Barnegat Bay, there are several channel edges and holes which reliably hold fluke.

boat in ever-widening circles until you locate a nice chunk of reef.

The spot marked by NJ #15, is not an artificial reef but is Shrewsbury Rock. This well-known hotspot is located at 40'20.74 x 73'57.20. You'll find that the bottom here rises all the way up to 15 feet, and is surrounded by 40 feet or so of water. As you might expect, flatfish can be found lurking around the edges of the structure, and even right on top of it at times.

NJ #16 marks the Sea Girt reef site. This is a large artificial reef with an eclectic collection of fish-attracting materials: several wrecks, artificial reef balls, rubble, and waste concrete have all been placed on this site. Start off at 40'07.71 x 73'55.60, but don't be afraid to move around here and explore a bit, as there's material scattered

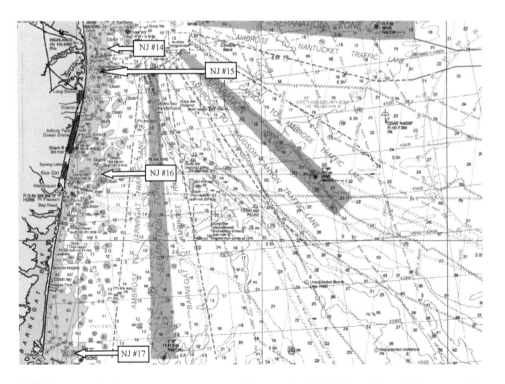

Off the coast, there are many wrecks and artificial reefs which provide an excellent shot at doormat-sized flatfish.

over a relatively wide area.

The spot at NJ #17, the Barnegat reef site, is just three miles off the beach and in nice weather, even relatively small boats should not have a problem getting here. It is located at 39'45.00 x 74'01.500.

Farther south along the coastline, the waters of Little Egg Harbor and Great Bay offer more prime fluke territory. Starting at NJ #18, behind Haven Beach, there's a hole that drops down to 18 feet of water and is surrounded by shallower sandy bottom. During an outgoing tide and low tides, try drifting minnow and minnow/squid combinations through this relatively deep water. As the tide begins to rise, shift over to the edges of the hole. When it's high, target flatfish on the shoals just outside of the deep water.

At the spots marked by NJ #19 (there are several of them,

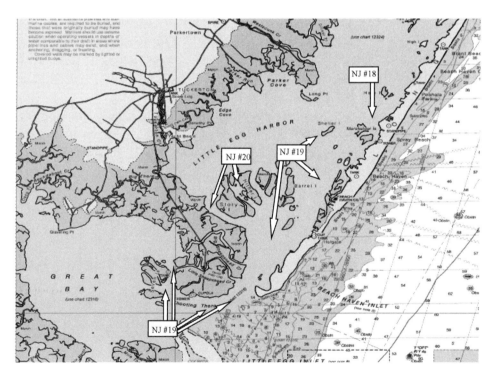

The south Jersey bays are full of fluke!

marked with two separate boxes and seven different arrows) you'll find deepwater channels (ranging from 25 to 45 feet deep) surrounded by shallower sandy flats. All of these channel edges are good places to apply the trolling and back-trolling techniques described earlier in this book. Drifting will also work well in these areas, but remember that you'll need a cooperative current and breeze that keeps you moving along the edges, not straight across, the channels—quite often, that's a tall order.

Both of the cuts marked by NJ #20, between Hither and Story Islands, offer nicely defined channels and fairly strong current when the tide is moving. Unlike some of the other channels marked by NJ #19, in these cuts, you're more likely to encounter edges that come up close to shore, and do not have large, sandy flats all around them. As a result, drifting close to the shoreline while bouncing leadheads with plastic tails, or bucktails, is a good mode of operation. When the tide dies out and water is low, these channels can still be worked by trolling through the deeper waters in the middle of the channel, but (as is usually the case when the current is dead or nearly dead) you can't expect the results to be as good.

The Ocean City reef site, at 39'10.50 x 74'33.500, marked by NJ #21, is another artificial reef hotspot that is fairly close to shore and accessible by small boats. This one lies four miles from the beach. Similarly, the Wildwood reef at NJ #22, which lies at 38'57.70 x 74'41.36, is also about four miles from land, and has plenty of wreckage scattered along the bottom to attract baitfish and predators. This reef site is also built around a large wreck, called the Gibson, which has provided a near-shore haven for fish for many years.

The spot at NJ #23 is much farther from the inlet, and accessing it will require a boat that can handle fairly long cruises through the ocean. Plug 38'58.50 x 74'11.00, and run for about 23 miles into the ocean. Appropriately, this spot is named the Deepwater Reef, and it lies in about 100 feet of water. This spot will be of more interest to anglers chasing sea bass and tautog (blackfish) so why should we flounder anglers take note? On beautiful summer weekend, the inshore and bay areas can become crowded with other boats. Many anglers would rather fish in seclusion, and on top of that, catches tend to be better when there's less competition all around you. And, even though it seems like an awful lot of water out here, it's not too deep for the flounder. So tuck this spot away in your back pocket for those weekends when all the boat traffic is driving you crazy, and you'd like to fish without other people all around.

The spot at NJ #24, the Cape May reef, sits at 38'52.03 x 74'41.45, and is much closer to home. This is a good reef site to remember, however. It's scattered over a large area, with depths ranging from 35' to 65'. That means trolling effectively, without requiring too many tight turns and sudden direction changes. If you're new to the sport and want to try experimenting with trolling for flounder for the first time, this would be a good area to try the tactic in a low-

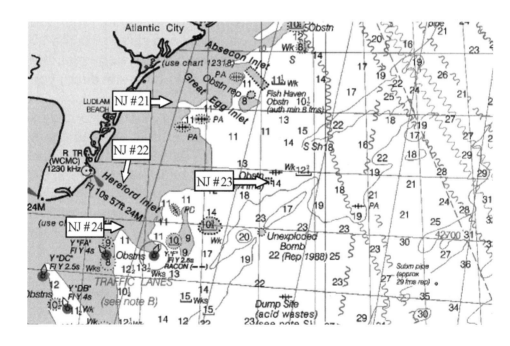

There are plenty of reefs and wrecks that hold flounder off of south Jersey, too.

pressure situation, since it's much easier to avoid tangles and similar problems when fewer tight turns are necessary.

There are many channels and deep water cuts running through the waters of Cape May. All have the potential to hold fluke, and those that are the most reliable are marked by the arrows of the NJ #25 hotspot. The usual inlet/channel tactics will apply, and all of these are fairly high-current areas. Also note NJ # 26, which points out a couple of inlet jetty hotspots. There's deep water at the end of the jetties of Cape May, and fluke can often be pulled out from the edges of it. The close to shore spot pointed out is good for a different reason; when a wind blows out of the north and the water becomes riled up and off-color, you can often locate a pocket of protected, calm water on this side of the inlet (and vise-versa, during a south

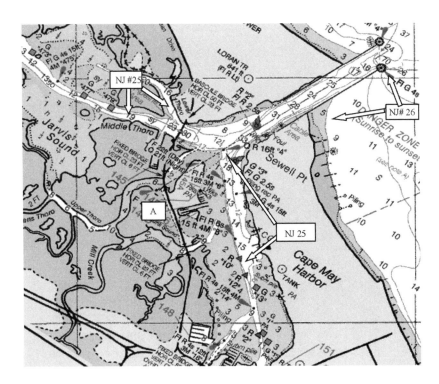

Cape May is famous for fluke!

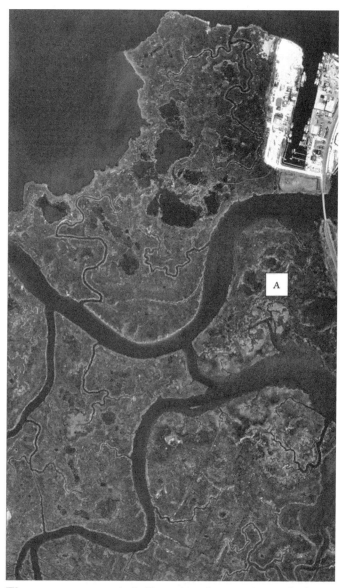

There are many twisting, turning cuts and channels behind Cape May—and all of them can hold
fluke! (Match the "A" in this photo with the "A" in
the previous chart.)

wind, though this area is much, much smaller). Use this as a back-up when you really want to fish, but weather conditions are making your normal game-plan unusable.

Famous for its outstanding fall striped bass fishery, the shoals near Cape May, New Jersey, also provide excellent fluke fishing opportunities. The same shoals and edges that attract and hold striped bass also bring in fluke. Just look at 'em all pointed out on the chart–Round Shoal (#27); North Shoal (#28); and Prissy Wicks Shoal (#29); Middle Shoal (#30); and one of the most famous, Over-falls Shoal (#31). The dramatic drops and holes, ranging from four feet to 35 feet within casting distance, in some areas, is clear to see. In addition to bottom structure galore, the shoals at the mouth of Delaware Bay are in an area of good current flow, which fluke find

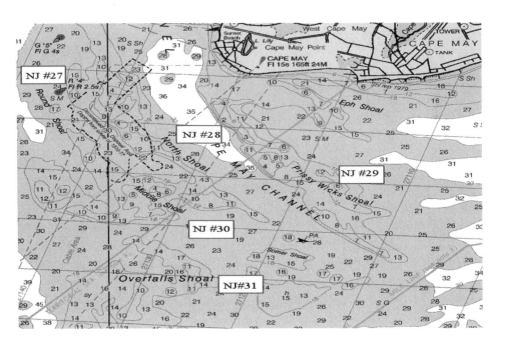

Cape May Shoals provide top-notch fluke action—just look at all of that structure!

very appealing. Visible rips are often clear to see, and the periods of strong current are long and often. Drifting long fluttering strip baits, and live baits, particularly spot, will bring lots of fluke strikes.

Note: Depending on wind speed and direction, and the phase of the moon, a strong current can create a considerable chop over these shoals. Visible rips are practically always clear to see, and when the currents, rips, and wind all collide this area can get ex-

Note the whitewater clearly visible even on this windless day, created by all the shoals and strong currents off of Cape May.

tremely hairy. In fact, the waters of Cape May Shoals have the potential to be some of the roughest described in this book, so be alert, and only tackle this water with a capable boat.

DELAWARE AND DELAWARE BAY

Much of the Delaware Bay consists of near-vertical shoals, sheer drop-offs, and strong currents. That means there's a lot for a fluke to like, about the Delaware.

As in most coastal states, Delaware's artificial reefs provide some good action. Reefs number six (DE #2) and seven (DE #3) are both located near Brown Shoal, DE #1. This shoal has been a traditional favorite among generations of Delaware Bay anglers, and for good reason, as for decades it has provided excellent fishing for seatrout, stripers and flounder. This productive shoal rises from depths of 40 feet up to 20 feet, then up to 15 feet, before coming within 10 feet of the surface. The current sweeps bait up and over, and all along Brown Shoal, and flounder take up ambush locations on the edges of the shoal.

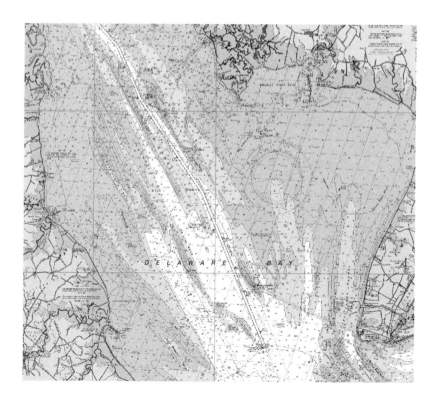

Brown Shoal has been enhanced by artificial reef site #6 and artificial reef site #7 that have been established near the shoal by the Delaware Artificial Reef Program. Reef site number six (DE #3 on our hotspot chart) consists of over 6,500 tons of concrete culverts and rubble, plus a 120' x 40' commercial barge called the Buccaneer. In all, the fish-attracting structure covers over a quarter of a square

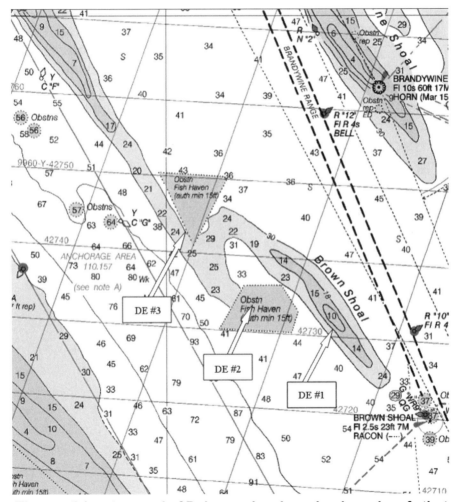

The south/eastern end of Delaware bay has shoals and reefs that flounder just love.

mile, with the location 38'57.90 x 75'09.60 right in the middle of the reef.

Reef number seven has over 8,000 tons of concrete, plus two small steel boats (the P3, 35 feet in length, and the Dolphin, 45 feet in length) and covers a slightly larger area. 38'56.60 x 75'08.60 will put you right in the middle of the reef site, but running the 38'56.50 line will take you over the bulk of the structure. These hard structure areas attract large fluke like a magnet. They can be caught directly on the reefs, and on the bottom immediately surrounding the reefs.

Put your boat in at the public ramp in Lewes, run down the Lewes/Rehoboth Canal to where it meets up with Delaware Bay, and hang a right toward the mouth of the bay. You won't miss the outer wall, as it's a long rock wall that rises well above the surface of the water. There's a shorter inner wall, then the longer outer wall. In October, anglers toggle into the outer wall and drop down crab baits for tautog on the rocks. In November and December, on the outer side (ocean side) of the wall, anglers drift eels in hopes of hooking up with striped bass. And from May through October, flounder are caught while drifting strip baits just outside of the outer wall. In this productive location, there's a hump that rises to 15 feet (DE #4,) plus other edges where the depth falls from 27 feet down to nearly 50 feet (DE #5 and #6,) and a visible rip will form when the current is strong.

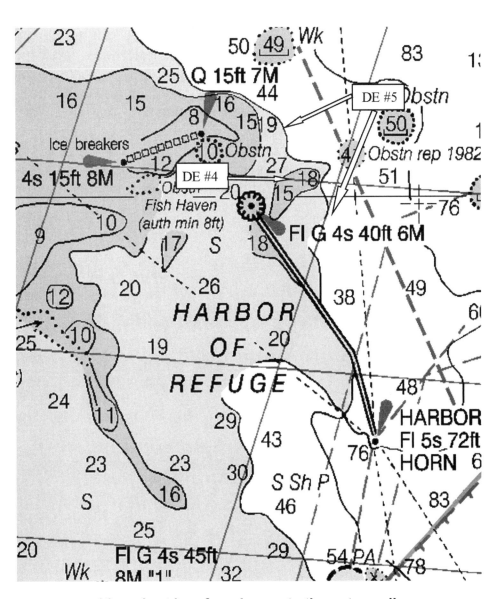

It's a short hop from Lewes to the outer wall.

During the heat of the summer, most big flounder are caught in deep water, and one of the most productive deep-water locations in Delaware Bay is at the edges of the anchorage. The anchorage is, in fact, an anchorage (for ships waiting to make their way up the bay,) and is delineated in this chart by the large rectangle, marked DE #7. Depths in the anchorage range from 60 to 100 feet, and the edges rise up to surrounding depths of 20 to 40 feet. Drifting on these edges and fishing depths of 50 to 80 feet is often very productive, especially in July and August. Eight, 10, and even 12 ounce sinkers may be

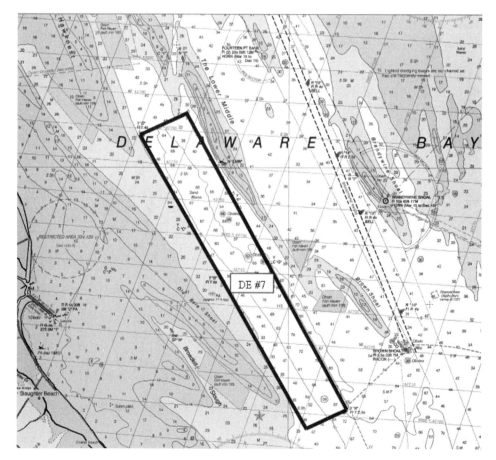

Head for the anchorage, during the dog days of summer.

needed to hold bottom in the deep water. Depending on the direction of the current, and direction of the wind, it may be necessary to run the motor and frequently re-position the boat so it maintains position over the most productive depth.

Depths in the vicinity of the Cross Ledge, marked by DE #9, vary from five feet to 44 feet. These significant bottom contours make the Cross Ledge a prime spot for flounder. When one or two fish are caught at a particular depth, you'll want to continue fishing that depth. Drift or troll along these edges, keeping a close eye on the depthfinder and using the motor as necessary to maintain position in the most productive depth range.

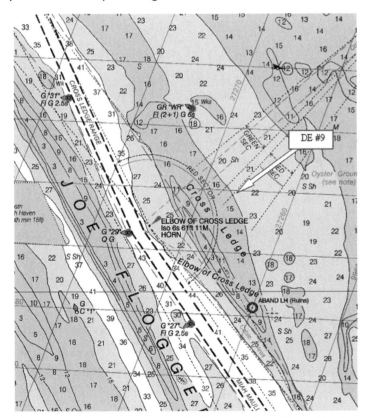

Cross Ledge is another Delaware Bay favorite for fluke hunters.

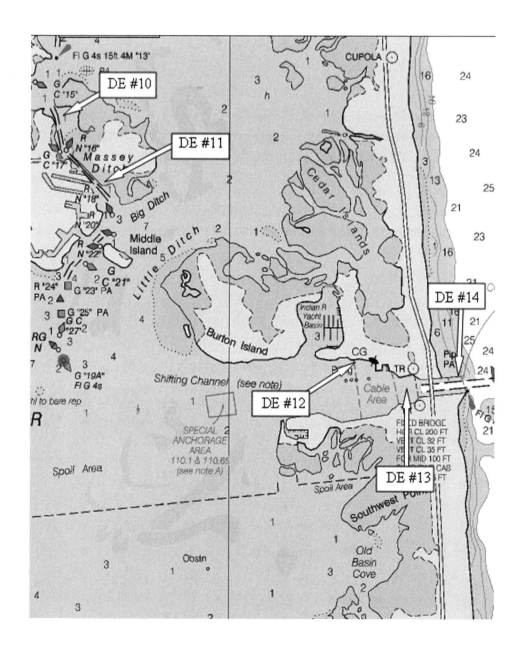

Indian River Inlet is Delaware's only coastal inlet—but it has excellent potential for flounder anglers. Inside of the inlet, at the channel below Bluff Point at DE #10, and the channel at Massy's Ditch, at DE #11, there's plenty of good fluke territory. Unfortunately, on sunny summer weekends there are also lots of fluke fishermen here. In fact the inlet and bay tend to become quite cramped through the peak of the season. So if you have lots of options, you may want to save fishing here for weekdays, or the spring and fall months.

If you fish the main inlet channel (marked by DE #13,) which many flounder anglers find a good spot to drift through with fluke killers baited with minnow/squid combinations, make sure you swing in close to the rip-rap rock wall marked by DE #12. There's plenty of very deep water here, down to 40 feet and more, which swirls around with confused currents as the moving water hits the edges. As you might expect, this confuses bait, which in turn brings in the flounder. DE #14 is important to note because this is a spot that should be checked out by anglers who are after fluke, but don't have a boat. It's possible to fish from the shoreline, from beyond the bridge all the way up to the jetty, and out on the jetty itself. If you choose to fish out on the jetty rocks, remember the dangers discussed earlier in this book, and the caution that must be used in this type of fishing. That said, the inlet and the jetty both support excellent fishing. Note that the current rips through the inlet here, and your rig is bound to be rolled along the bottom no matter how much weight you use. Accordingly, stick with sinkers that will snag as little as possible, and tie them to your rig with light line, so you can break them off and at least get part of your rig back, when the weight snags. Remember: this is part of fishing jetties; you have to plan on losing gear.

MARYLAND AND MARYLAND'S CHESAPEAKE BAY

With the Chesapeake Bay to the west and the Atlantic coast to the east, Maryland has very diverse fishing opportunities. Both inland and coastal anglers chase flatfish in this state, and the varying conditions can make it seem like entirely different fisheries—in one case you'll be fighting strong currents, and in the other, you'll be

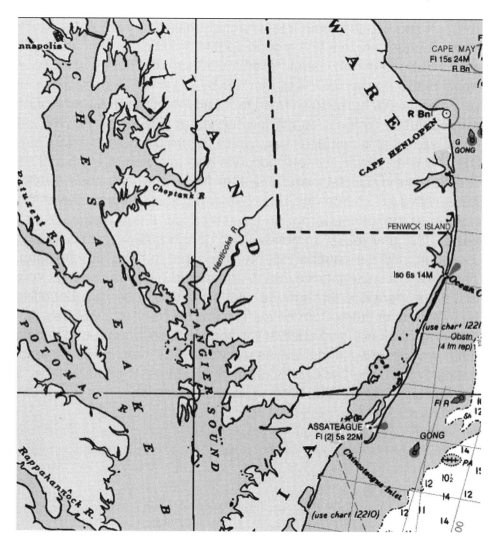

wishing for them. And, in either case, hopefully, you'll feel a flounder or two or 10 on the end of your line.

Ocean City is an area that, like Delaware Bay, sees more than its fair share of traffic through the summer months. In fact, this is one of the most heavily traveled, heavily fished coastal bays on the east coast. Still, it provides plenty of opportunity, especially during the week and during the off-season.

The first spot to note, MD #1, is a channel area running through the very shallow bay, commonly known as the Thoroughfare. It should be noted that the charts in this book should not be used for navigation, and even though the chart included here is NOAA's latest version of the area, the channels and shoals in this bay have shifted since the chart's publication. (In fact, some temporary channel markers are currently in place, several yards away from the old ones, because the channels and shoals shifted just in the past year!)

In any case, the deeper channels of the Thoroughfare area are one of the most popular areas to fluke fish in Ocean City. Drifting squid or squid/minnow along the edges is the standard practice, and anglers will also do well jigging with leadheads dressed with soft plastic tails.

MD #2 is another area that sees plenty of anglers, the channel running along the bulkhead behind Ocean City. There are plenty of fish in there but the important thing to remember when drifting this channel is to look out for the large party and tour boats coming through, when the drawbridge opens up. They are limited to a fairly tight channel here, and if anglers don't stay out of their way, things can get hairy!

The Rt. 50 bridge, marked by MD #3, is not only a great area for boat anglers, it's also one of the best areas around for shorebound anglers. Anyone can park and walk out onto the bridge catwalk for free, at any time of the year, and fish from the bridge. The catwalk is fenced and secure, and has plenty of room for a multitude of anglers. It's fairly high off the water, so a bridge net (a hoop net with a weight in the middle, to keep it upright, which is lowered from the bridge) is very helpful when landing fluke from the catwalk.

The arrows on this chart point to two spots along the bridge where channels run through. The one to the right is the main channel, and the one to the left is smaller but no less productive. Plan to fish around the channel edges during low and falling tides, and up on the shoals between them during the high tides. Most anglers fishing from the bridge stick with baited top and bottom rigs. The pier "trolling" tactic noted earlier (walking down the pier with your rod in-hand) is very effective here when the crowds are thin enough to allow it.

MD #4 covers the inlet itself. Fewer numbers of fluke are caught right in the inlet, but those that are caught here are commonly very large fish. Most sharpies working this area will stick with relatively large (four to six inch) live baits such as spot, which attract the lunker flounder to the hook.

MD #5, the inlet jetty, is another spot for shoreline anglers to keep in mind. Like the Indian River jetty it requires walking out on rocks, however, you can also fish from the sidewalk just inside of the jetty. You will tend to hook bottom more often, as you'll be reeling in your lines at a greater angle (and dragging the weights across the rip-rap) but it's a much safer bet if you're fishing with kids, or just don't want to risk a walk on the rocks. Also, as with Indian River, come with lots of extra gear and plan to lose lots of weights and rigs.

The sheer drop-off from 12 feet to 60 feet of water, west of Poplar Island, is the northernmost reliable flounder hotspot in the Maryland portion of the Chesapeake. This hotspot, marked by MD #6, is very easy to locate thanks to the red channel marker number 84, to the west of the island. All of the flatfish migrating into Eastern Bay and other points to the north will gather along and move across this edge during the late spring, usually some time between mid to late May and mid June. During this time frame, you can make good catches by drifting down this edge when there is either a north, south, or dead wind. If there's a west or east breeze don't focus on this spot, because you will blow up or down the edge so quickly it will be essentially impossible to fish it. The drop is so sheer that sometimes the bow of your boat will be in 20 feet of water, and the stern will be in 30. So it's incredibly important to be able to drift up and down the

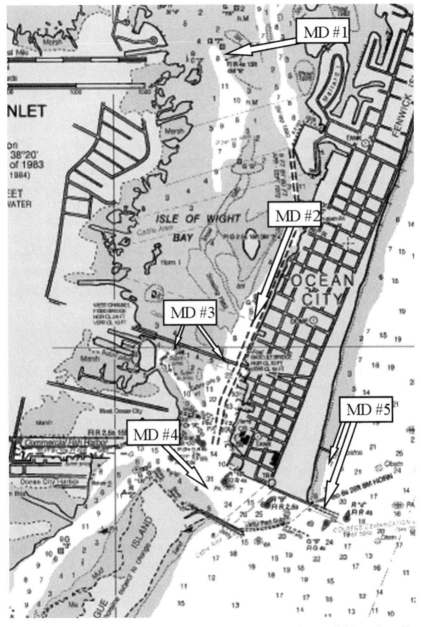

Ocean City makes up the coastal bay portion of Maryland's flounder fishery.

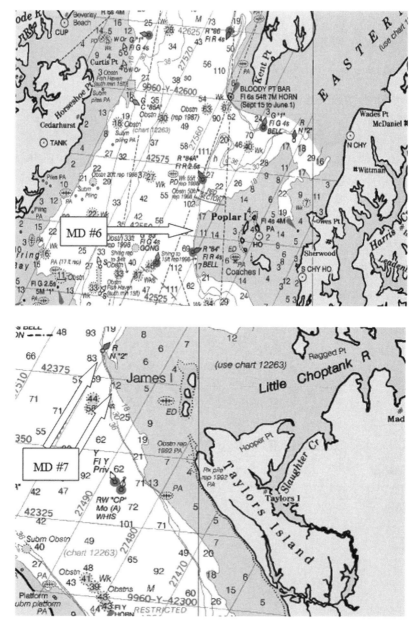

The northern area of Maryland's portion of the Chesapeake is particularly hot for a two to three week period during the late spring.

shelf, as opposed to across it. Drift anchors (drogues) will help if the wind is gentle but otherwise, don't invest a lot of time in getting here.

Also, not that there will often be a line of crab pots along the top of this shelf. Use these crab pots to help determine the exact spot you are drifting in, and it will be easy to return to the exact location along the shelf where you found the fish.

MD #7 marks a spot off the mouth of the Little Choptank River, which is another spring hotspot. Some seasons flounder will be caught here through here summer and fall, but usually not in large enough numbers to make them the target fish. As with the edge at marker 84, mid May through mid June is the prime time. Also like MD #6, this spot is easy to locate thanks to a marker. There is a red nun buoy #2 which marks the northern edge of this drop-off. Unlike the other hotspot, however, the edge is more erratic and is not nearly as steep. So, it's possible to fish effectively here in most conditions.

MD #8 is a general area, as opposed to a specific hotspot: the Tangier Sound. Just east of Smith Island, the sound and the town of Crisfield offer excellent access (there's a public ramp right in the heart of town) to some awesome waters, filled with oodles of edges, lumps and other bottom contours, as you can see on the chart. There are shallow spots from seven and eight feet deep, to the deepest locations which drop down to more than 60 and even 70 feet – just the type of uneven bottom that flounder love.

Across the bay at MD #9, Cornfield Harbor, just south of Point Lookout, Maryland, lies at the mouth of the Potomac River. It features a hook-shaped sandbar that on one side has depths of three to five feet, while just on the other side of the bar the bottom falls off sharply to depths of 13, 27 and 35 feet. In addition to the pronounced bottom structure, there's good current flow through here, making Cornfield

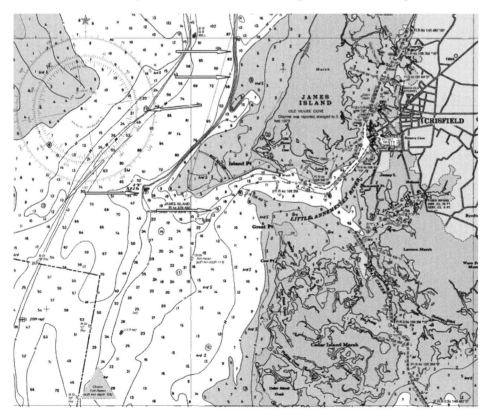

Harbor an excellent flounder fishing location.

MD #10 is another hotspot shoreline anglers should remember. Flounder are caught by anglers on the Point Lookout Pier. Fishing the deeper water at the end of the pier, which is 10 feet deep, with live shiners and minnows, especially in the evening and early-morning hours, will produce flounder. There is also a causeway leading into the park, at MD #11, which is very popular with shoreline anglers. Note, however, that during the summer months it can become jam-packed with anglers on weekends, and an early arrival is necessary to stake out a spot along this causeway.

MD #12 marks the Mud Leads. Although the drop-offs here are not as steep as those found in many other parts of the bay, this is a heavy feeding zone for many species of fish. As a result there's often a good deal of feeding action here, and the fluke can be found patiently waiting below, for the natural results of a feeding frenzy. Since the fish will usually be scattered across this area as opposed to holding on a particular edge, plan on trolling during calm conditions, when the drift would be slow—you'll want to cover lots of territory.

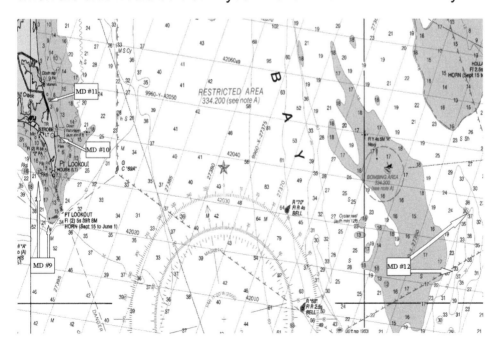

VIRGINIA AND VIRGINIA'S CHESAPEAKE

Anglers from Virginia, North Carolina, Maryland, Delaware, Pennsylvania, New Jersey and beyond travel to the seaside of Virginia's Eastern Shore every year to enjoy its famous early spring flounder fishing action. Virginia's Eastern Shore is just below Ocean City, Maryland, beginning at Assateague and continuing south to Cape Charles and the Chesapeake Bay Bridge Tunnel. The most popular springtime flounder fishing destination on the Eastern Shore is Wachapreague, Virginia.

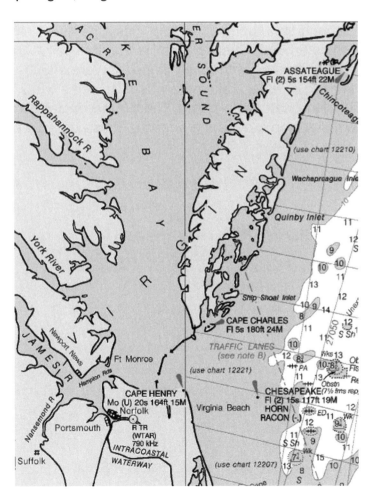

The early run of fish here, usually beginning some time around the first week of April, sees many large doormats. Later in the spring and through the fall flatties will be caught here in large numbers, though the bulk of the catch will be more average sized fish. Nice flounder are caught throughout the channels and guts, yet the most popular hot spot is often Drawing channel, at VA #2. The Hummock, at VA #1, is another good bet, which is significantly less popular. There's a channel running into the mud flats at VA #3, right next to a small marsh island, which is an excellent spot to try as the tide is falling. Both the drop-off next to the island and the channel edge across from it are productive areas. If the tide is high, however, move up onto the mud flats themselves and enjoy the finest shallow-water fluke fishing around. Casting light jigs and bucktails—particularly white bucktails trimmed with squid strips—is very effective here, in just a foot or two of water. Take note when you see a white PVC pole sticking out of the water in this area. These mark oyster bars, and the flounder will stack up around the edges of these bars on flood tides to feed.

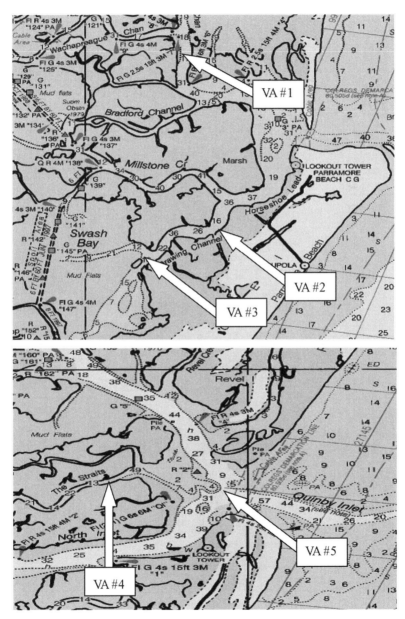

Wachapreague, Virginia, is one of the most popular early season flatfish destinations in the area, but Quinby is also an excellent destination.

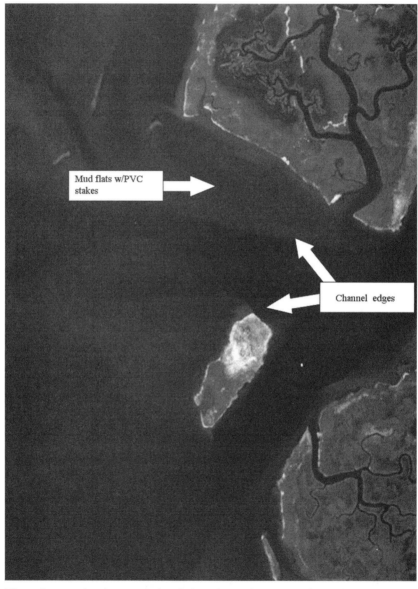

The channel edges at the island, and across from it, are both productive. On a flood tide, move up onto the mud flats and look for PVC stakes, indicating oyster bars.

In addition to Wachapreague, there's also outstanding flounder action in April and May each year at Quinby. The main channel,
which hits a shoal at VA #4, is always a good bet. There's also reliable
fishing in the Straits, marked by VA #5. Folly's Creek, Chincoteague,
and other seaside locations along Virginia's beautiful Eastern Shore
also have good flounder action.

Farther north and west, along the Eastern Shore side of the
Chesapeake Bay, lies Windmill Point. The point extends well away
from shore under water, and creates wonderful drop-offs both on the
north and south sides, as shown by VA #6. Choose which side of the
point to fish according to the tide. On an incoming tide, you're likely
to find better action on the south side of the bar. On an outgoing,
however, the north side will usually be the main producer.

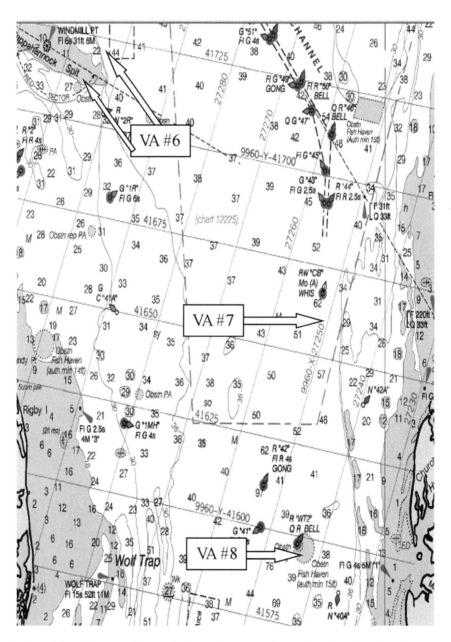

In the Virginia portion of the Chesapeake, there's plenty of action for flounder fishermen.

Farther south and on the eastern side of the bay lay VA #7, and #8. The commonwealth of Virginia has created an artificial reef known as the Cell. This spot is marked off as VA #8, and it attracts a wide variety of fish, including spadefish, seatrout, croaker, cobia, red drum, tautog and—of course—big, fat flounder. Live baits, and leadheads dressed with plastics (such as Bass Assassins), can be fished on and in the hard structure at the Cell. Flounder can also be caught while drifting strip baits in the 30 to 60 foot depths just north of the Cell, in the area marked off by VA #7.

In the middle of the Chesapeake, just off the York Spit Channel, there's an area known as "The Hump" (VA #9 on our hotspot chart) which is another favorite location for flounder fishermen. The Hump rises from 35 and 33 feet of water up to within 27 feet of the surface, and its edges hold flounder. Flounder are also caught by anglers drifting the 30 foot depths all around The Hump.

Slightly southwest at a spot called Bluefish Rock, the depths vary from 29 to 24 to 20 feet, and there are some two bumps that rise to within 16 feet of the surface. While Bluefish Rock is famous for the big cobia it produces each season, it's also a very productive location for flounder pounders. Drifting strip baits and live baits such as spot over these bottom contours turns up impressive catches of flounder every year.

As its name suggests, the Chesapeake Bay Bridge Tunnel features both bridge sections, and tunnel sections. The tunnels are on the bottom of the bay, providing an "open" section on the surface of the water in the bridge-tunnel complex, enabling big ships to sail over the submerged tunnels and between the above-water bridge sections. (Ships are too big, tall and wide to travel under the bridge sections and through the bridge pilings.) Big boulder "islands" were created at the beginning and end of each of the two tunnels, for a total of four islands. Big boulders were also placed on top of and around the tunnels to stabilize them on the bottom.

There are two tunnels and four "islands" on the Chesapeake Bay Bridge Tunnel, and the islands are counted from south (Virginia Beach side) to north (Cape Charles/Eastern Shore side). Claude Bain, Director of the Virginia Saltwater Fishing Tournament and a local sharpie, has provided a number of Chesapeake Bay locations that consistently produce big flounder; he has identified the area around the third and fourth islands as a significant flounder hot spot. The Chesapeake channel runs between them, and this area is marked off as VA #11.

The specialized rockpile drifting and rockpile trolling techniques described in chapter seven will catch flounder on the submerged boulders on and around the underwater tunnels. Drifting over the tunnels and between the islands, or trolling along the rockpiles from one island toward the other, will also produce flounder. Plenty of flounder are pulled from the boulders each season, including lots of eight, nine, and 10 pound fish, and some even larger!

Whenever possible, fish the ends of the islands. There's little current and few fish along the sides of the islands, so avoid these areas. Instead, fish the northern and southern ends, where the current smacks the rocks and becomes diverted and confused. Also concentrate your efforts where the tunnel goes down or where the bridge starts, and work from there to the bridge pilings. Fish the pilings too—lots of flounder are caught right next to them.

Another flounder hot spot along the Chesapeake Bay Bridge Tunnel is very near Fisherman's Island on the Eastern Shore side, at

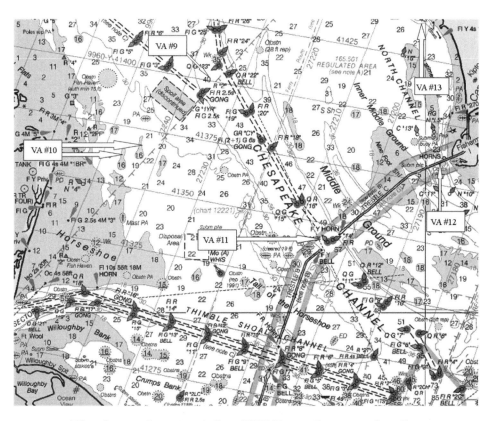

The lower bay and the CBBT are famous for the incredible fishing.

what is known as the High Level Bridge area of the complex, at VA #12. Sharp edges and other bottom contours attract and hold plenty of flounder each season, and drifters do very well at this location.

There is also very good lower Chesapeake Bay flounder fishing at VA #13, straight out from the town of Cape Charles on the Eastern Shore. Flounder are caught all along the ledge where the bottom drops from about 20 feet down to 60 feet. The long ledge runs from off Cape Charles south to Old Plantation Flats all the way down to the concrete ships at the Kiptopeke boat ramp. This is a long, long feature, and the fish may be found congregated anywhere along the drop-off. Drift strip baits, run the motor to control the drift, and re-position the boat as necessary to keep the boat directly over the ledge and the baits in the strike zone.

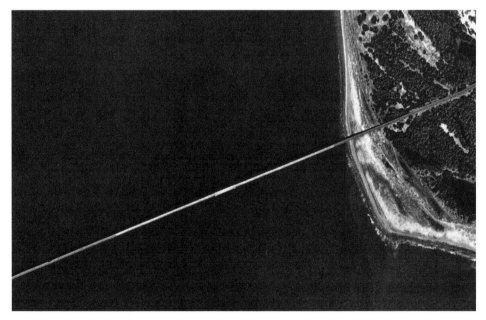

The CBBT goes across islands, dives under the bay, and spans the water from above.

Bain suggests that if you'd like more information on Virginia flounder fishing hot spots and techniques, write to: Virginia Saltwater Fishing Tournament, Virginia Marine Resources Commission, 968 South Oriole Drive, Suite 102, Virginia Beach, VA 23451. Or, call (757) 491-5160.

NORTH CAROLINA

North Carolina is an angler's haven, no doubt about it. Whether you're on foot, in a truck, or in a boat there are plenty of hotspots for you to hit that will produce flounder galore.

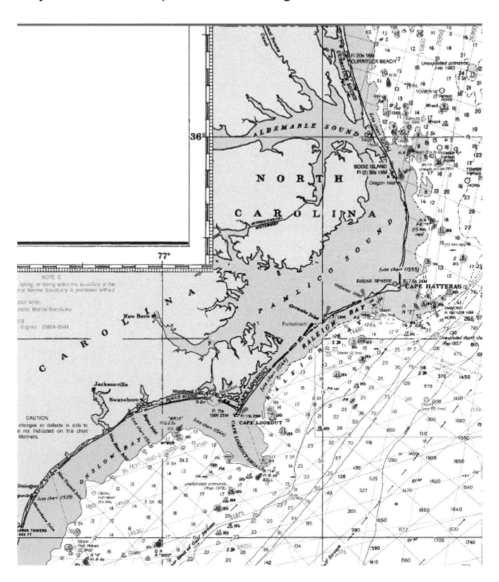

The sound inside of Oregon Inlet is a shallow bay with few features other than the channels. So, as one might expect, the best flounder fishing generally occurs near or on these edges. When fishing the bay here, simply go to an area such as NC #1, find that edge, and fish along it from channel marker to channel marker. Note that even inside of the channel depths will rarely drop below eight or 10 feet, so light gear is in order here. In fact, with an ultralight fishing rod rigged up with eight or 10 pound test braid or superline, one can bounce quarter- and half-ounce jigs and small bucktails along the bottom very effectively. NC #2 indicates the mouth of the inlet itself, which holds plenty of fish. As with the rest of the bay, the trick here is to simply locate the channel edges. Anglers without boats, however, will also be very interested in this inlet. There's vehicular beach access here, and one can drive right out to the surf and the inlet in any four-wheel drive truck. That makes this area a top pick for surf anglers who want to fish for flounder, as well as other species.

The northern side of the inlet is an excellent place to try casting bucktails trimmed with squid strips, of four-inch twister tail jigs, in search of flounder. Give this a shot, especially during an incoming tide, and you have an excellent shot at scoring. There's also a pond which forms here sometimes, on the western edge of the tip of the beach. It comes and goes through the years, as storms carve it out and then fill it back in. There's no guarantee it'll be here on any given spring, but if you fish in this area keep an eye out, and if the pond is present, be sure to take a few casts into it. Sometimes it's fruitless, and others, it seems as though every fish in North Carolina has crowded into one small area to feed.

At NC #3 you'll find the AR-130, an artificial reef site made up mostly of old boxcars, plus concrete reef balls, pipes, and the prerequisite rubble. This site is a good 12 miles north of the inlet at 36'00.19 x 75'31.88, so it'll take some cruising to get there, but the distance from the inlet ensures less competition than one might expect.

NC #4 is another offshore wreck site, this one located at 35'43.80 x 75'26.78. It's called the Oregon Inlet Reef, or AR-160, and it sits four miles from the inlet. This reef has a lot of material

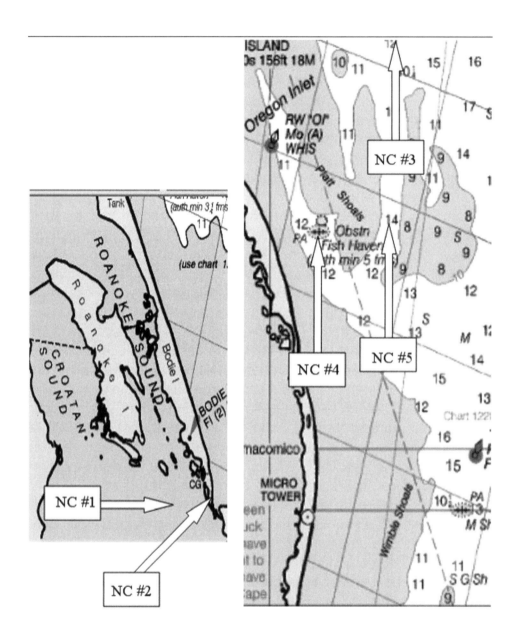

Oregon Inlet, North Carolina's northernmost inlet, has great angling opportunities.

planted on it: several 400 foot long liberty ships, a trawler, concrete rubble, reef balls, and pipes. One of the Liberty ships is called the Zane Gray, so many people refer to this site as the Zane Gray site. As you might at other reef sites, try to fish right along the edges of the structure to find the fluke. Mark your hotspots with a float marker, and after you find a fish or two, work the area thoroughly before moving on.

The site at NC #5 is not a reef site, but a natural slough running through the bottom. It's commonly known as and the "First Slough" and the bottom here varies from the upper 40's to the lower 60's. As you might expect, flounder will move in along the edges of these drops to feed starting in the spring and running through the summer.

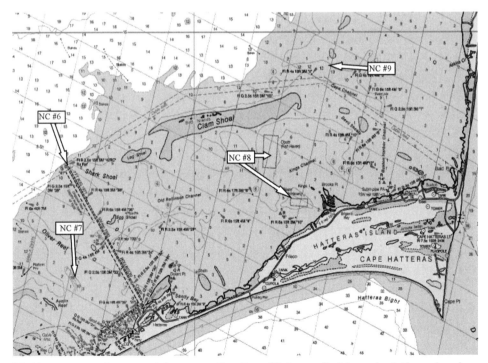

Hatteras may be most famous for its offshore fishing, but there's also great fluke action in the back bay!

Behind Hatteras there's also some excellent flatfish territory. This first hotspot to note is the channel running past Shark Shoal. The surrounding areas are shallow and are riddled with shoals and sand bars (don't try cutting channel markers in this neck of the woods!) so much as it is to the north, fishing the channel edges is usually a good bet. The hole at NC #6 does, however, have some notable deeper water. When the tide has run out and is nearly or completely low, hit this hole and you may find the fish concentrated tightly.

NC #8 marks a pair of reefs, which are most often fished by anglers going for sheepshead, croaker, and speckled sea trout. However, just like to offshore reef sites, drifting fluke killer rigs baited with the minnow/squid combo or a long, fluttering strip bait, is often effective for flounder in the same area.

Just to the north at NC #9, there's a nice drop off to 12 feet, with the channel on one side and a flat to the other. Fish along this edge on an incoming tide, and drop back to the deeper sections and the near-by channel, during the outgoing and low tides.

Outside of Hatteras Inlet, at NC #10, is another artificial reef, this one made of a tug and a freighter wreck. It can be found at 35'06.18 x 75'42.97, ands is called AR-230. NC #11 offers more of the same, though this reef (at 35'08.10 x 75'40.56) also has reef balls and rubble.

NC# 12 isn't a specific reef or spot, so much as a general mark for Diamond Shoals. This entire area can be productive, as it sees shoals, drop-offs, and rigorous currents throughout the area. It should be noted, however, that although this area can be incredibly productive it can also be incredibly dangerous; plan on trying this area during calm weather, and look out for visible rips.

NC #13 marks another wreck, this one called the Australia, a 510 foot long tanker which was torpedoed in World War II. This is a significant chunk of structure and it lies in fairly deep (85 to 100 foot deep) waters. Bottom fishing here won't usually produce large numbers of flatfish (note, however, that there are tons of sea bass in the area) but the flounder it does produce will generally be very large ones. If you want to target doormats in the middle of the season, this spot would be a good bet.

NC #14 marks Bogue Inlet. Both in the inlet and in the creeks, cuts and channels behind it, flounder abound. Most of the bottom inside the inlet area here is sandy and full of long flats, but if you stick to the channel edges and treat these waters as you would the other back bays in North Carolina, by casting and retrieving with relatively light gear, you have a great shot at flounder. At NC #15, however, it's back to heavy weights and deep water. This spot marks the Atlantic Beach Reef, AR 315, at 34.40 x 33 x 76'44.67. This is another biggie, with liberty ships, trawlers, rubble, and many other items planted on the bottom to bring in the fish.

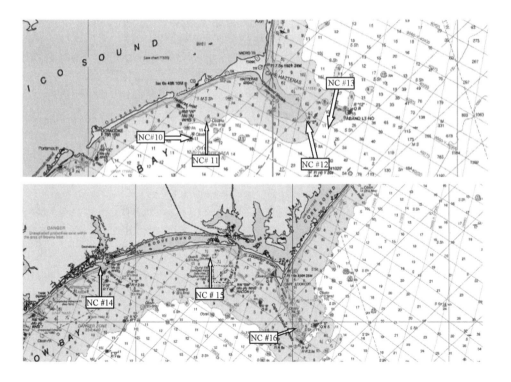

The waters outside of the inlets are also rich in fish.

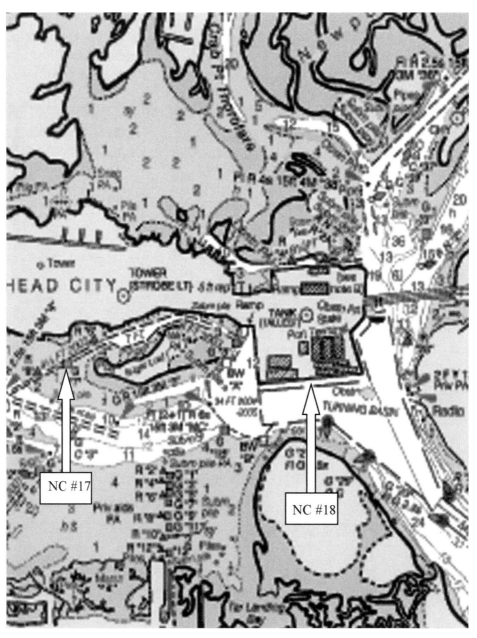

Morehead City sees occasional run of gigantic, doormat fluke.

NC #16, the Cape Lookout shoals, should be approached just like the cape Hatteras shoals. This is productive water full of shoals, drops and rips, and it's also unpredictable and somewhat dangerous, especially for inexperienced boaters.

The NC #17 hotspot is, like so many in the North Carolina coastal bay areas, simply a channel running through sandy shoals and flats. Through most of the bay here, drifting these channel edges will produce fish. Hotspot NC #18, however, is unique. The long, flat wall shown here is a seawall, at a commercial unloading dock. Sometimes you won't be able to fish here, because ships will be in for unloading cargo, or to load phosphorus from the pier. When there isn't a ship tied up here, however, there is often excellent flounder fishing right along this seawall. Simply drop down top/bottom rigs, and drift along right next to it. In the past several years, some significant runs of extremely large flatfish have developed here, and these jumbo fish are almost always taken from right alongside the seawall.

Of course, flounder can be caught in bays and near-shore hotspots all they way down to Florida, and around the Gulf Coast. The most effective tactics, baits, and methods of taking these fish in their southern range do tend to vary, and anglers don't focus on them nearly as often in areas like Florida as we might in Maryland, Delaware, or other Mid Atlantic states. The tactics and techniques covered in this book thus far will serve you well in the Mid Atlantic region and may well work as you get south of the areas covered here, but for the purposes of this book, North Carolina will be considered our southernmost point of coverage.

CHAPTER 11

FLOUNDER DELIGHT—IN SEARCH OF THE PERFECT MEAL

Now, are you ready for a prime dinner? Ensuring perfect-tasting fish begins the moment you bring a flounder into the boat.

KEEP 'EM COLD

Fluke that meet or exceed minimum size requirements will usually be going home for dinner. They get deposited in a cooler, where it's very important to keep them cold. One way is to fill a large cooler with ice chips, and bury fluke in the chips so they're completely surrounded on all sides by ice. Occasionally drain the cooler of water from ice that has melted. Ice melts considerably slower when water is removed. Water is warmer than ice (or it would be ice), and the warmer water will speed the melting of the ice, so remember to drain that cooler.

I have read, and have had fishing experts tell me, that the absolute best way to keep flounder (and other fish) ice cold in a cooler is to put in a block of ice along with some chipped ice. Then add some saltwater, then dump in some kosher salt. The resulting brine will fall below 32-degrees, yet will not freeze because of the high salt content. The flounder go into the water, which is kept at freezing temperatures by the ice block and salt.

If you fail to keep the flounder at minimal temperatures, the taste will be noticeably affected. That makes chilling your catch an important part of fluke fishing. Proper storage and maintenance of flounder will keep the flesh firm and in perfect shape for fine dining!

FILLETING FLOUNDER

Other than perhaps cleaning the boat, rinsing the tackle, and filling in your log book, filleting fluke comes at the very end of a fishing trip, the very end of the day, when you're tired, hot, and thirsty. However, you need to keep your focus so you fillet 'em right and you, your family, and friends are rewarded with delicious fluke dinners.

Always use a sharp, top-quality thin-bladed knife. Sharpen it several times during the filleting process, if necessary. A sharp knife is always much safer than a dull knife, as a dull knife requires lots of pressure to cut, which can lead to dangerous slips and accidents. Use knives that feature non-slip handles. Use a cutting board or fishing-cleaning station that features a surface on which the fluke won't slide much. Keep it clean by wiping it down or washing it off with water, after every fish if necessary.

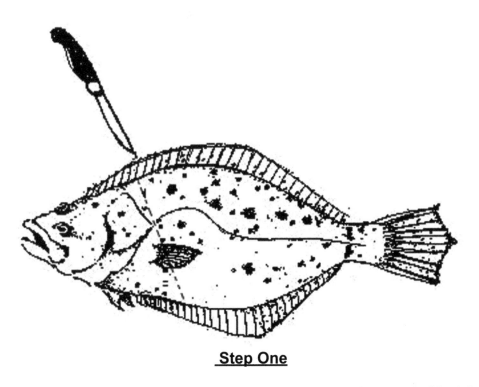

Step One

The first cut is diagonal, from high behind the head, down behind the fin, down to just behind the gut area. You're filleting just the top side of the flounder, so the cut should only be as deep as the backbone (do not cut through the backbone into the other side of the fish).

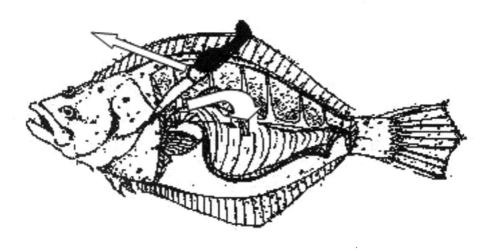

Step Two

Make second cut across tail, only down to the backbone. Slide the knife blade into the second cut so the blade is along the backbone and facing toward the top of the fish. Using the rib cage as a guide, firmly and smoothly work the knife forward on the fish and toward the long fin along the top of the flounder, until the blade reaches the first cut. Be careful not to cut thought the ribs, as you do so. This will slice the meat from the rib cage.

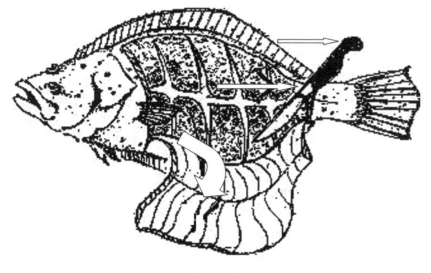

Step Three

The top half of the first fillet will now be separated from the fish. Lift it, insert the knife blade, and slice down (to the long bottom fin) and backward (to the tail) on the fish. Cut along the fin and tail to remove entire fillet from fish. The top of the fluke is now filleted.

Flip the fish and repeat this same process on the white side. You'll then have two firm fillets that are ready to be skinned (some people leave the skin on which is cooked and eaten with the fillet). Note that while the white (down) side of the flounder is not as meaty, the fillets you get from this portion of the fish are just as tasty as the thicker fillets from the flounder's back.

DELICIOUS RECIPES FROM CHEF DAVID HAINES

Some 15 years ago, while we were arranging a fishing trip, my friend told me not to worry about lunches, as a buddy he was bringing along would provide the lunches. It turned out to be the best I have ever eaten while on the water! The prime rib sandwiches were spectacular, a far cry from the peanut butter and jelly or baloney sandwiches I usually throw together for myself.

The buddy who brought them was David Haines. Make that Chef David Haines. David has earned a reputation as an outstanding chef while preparing and serving countless fabulous meals and banquets as Chef at the Harmony Inn, D & S Brasserie, Meadia Heights Golf Club, Bent Creek Country Club, Distinctive Affairs Catering and Michael's Casual Dining in Lancaster and south-central Pennsylvania.

Now, 15 years after that first fishing trip, just by chance, David and I work together at the Solanco School District in southern Lancaster County. David is Director of Food Services, and the improvements in our school lunches and school banquets have been remarkable. David is always welcome to fish with me on my boat—especially when he offers to bring lunch!

I asked David to provide a few of his favorite flounder recipes for publication in this book. Not content to write them down, David invited me and Tom Stauffer (another Solanco fisherman) over to his place so he could demonstrate each recipe, and so we could enjoy a couple of cold beverages while we tasted each flounder dish for ourselves. They were quick and easy to prepare, and absolutely delicious. Use David's recipes and treat yourself to mouth-water meals following a successful day of flounder fishing.

Impress your fishing buddies, family, friends and co-workers with these fabulous flounder recipes from Chef David Haines!

Chef David Haines dips a flounder fillet in egg wash.

Flounder Roulades

Prepare crabmeat mixture:
1 pound crabmeat (lump)
1 egg, beaten
2 teaspoons mayonnaise (Hellman's)
1 teaspoon lemon juice
Old Bay seasoning to taste
3 pieces of bread crust cut off and cut into 1/2-inch cubes (use white bread)
1/2 teaspoon mustard
1/2 teaspoon chopped parsley

Lay flounder fillet flat and spread crabmeat mixture over fillet
Roll fillet (like a jelly roll)
Put two rolled fillets with crabmeat mixture into individual greased baking dishes
Put a dap of butter on top and sprinkle with Old Bay
Bake at 325 degrees for about 20 minutes

To take this dish over the top, try adding burre blanc cream sauce:

3 tablespoons dry sherry
1/2 cup dry white wine
2 tablespoons chopped shallot
Heat above ingredients to boil and allow to boil until volume is reduced by half, then add:
2 tablespoons heavy cream
1-1/2 sticks unsalted butter cut into small pieces
Pour over flounder roulades and enjoy!

Baked Flounder with Ritz Crackers

Brush fillets with a butter blend
Roll flounder in course Ritz cracker crumbs
Spray baking dish with Pam
Bake at 350 degrees for about 18 minutes
It's really that easy!

Pan Fried Flounder

Squeeze a little lemon juice onto the flounder fillets
Dust fillets with flour
Dip in egg wash (egg and cream or milk)
Put in hot buttered frying pan
Cook on both sides until lightly brown

The following Mediterranean goes perfectly with pan fried flounder—
try it out for yourself, you'll agree!

1 stick butter
1/2 cup sliced mushroom
1/2 cup chopped fresh tomato (skin and seeds removed)
1/2 cup dried shallot
1 clove garlic
2 teaspoons capers
Melt butter; sauté the above ingredients
(Sauce can be kept warm until the fried flounder is finished)
Serve over pan-fried flounder

ENJOY!

IN CONCLUSION

I hope this book has been an interesting and easy read for you. More importantly, whether you're relatively new to flounder fishing or an experienced veteran, my hope is that this book features at least several tactics, techniques and other information you are now able to use to effectively locate and catch more flounder, more often.

Fluke fishing is a challenging, exciting, rewarding sport. There's always more to learn as we strive to better understand our quarry so we can become more consistently successful flounder fishermen. Make each trip a learning experience. Enjoy every fishing trip, especially your family and friends you fish with!

GOOD LUCK!

ABOUT THE AUTHOR

In 1989, Keith Kaufman was hired as Managing Editor of *The Fisherman* magazine, Mid Atlantic Edition in Lewes, Delaware. He served in that position for a decade, which provided him opportunities to fish with, and learn from, some of the very best fishermen along the entire Atlantic coast and beyond.

Keith, his wife Stephanie, and their sons Cody and Ross now live in Lancaster County, Pennsylvania, where Keith works as Director of Communications for the Solanco School District. Each season, he trailers his Starcraft Fishmaster 196 from one end of Chesapeake Bay to the other—from Susquehanna Flats south to Cape Charles, Virginia—where Keith, his sons and friends catch striped bass, black and red drum, cobia, spadefish, croaker, bluefish, and especially flounder. Keith's fishing experience also includes tarpon, snook, redfish, seatrout, king salmon and other species from Costa Rica to Florida to Delaware Bay to Lake Ontario, and lots of locations in between.

Keith is currently field editor for *The Fisherman* magazine, a regular contributor for *Chesapeake Angler* magazine, an outdoor correspondent for the *Reading Eagle* newspaper, and a popular speaker at fishing seminars and outdoor shows. His extensive writing experience also includes how-to, where-to fishing stories, fishing reports, product review columns, advertising copy and marine fisheries conservation articles that have been published by Bass Pro Shops, *Big Game Fishing Journal, Pennsylvania Game News,* and several fishing-oriented websites.

Keith was the recipient of the 1998-1999 Mid Atlantic Conservation Media Award from the Coastal Conservation Association, Virginia Chapter. He graduated with honors with a Bachelor of Arts Degree in Communications from East Stroudsburg University in Pennsylvania.

This is Keith's second book. His first, *Fishing for Weakfish,* was published by The Fisherman Library in 2000.

Rudow's Guide To

FISHING THE MID ATLANTIC

38 Charts with More Than **300** Hot Spots!

COASTAL BAYS & OCEAN

By Lenny Rudow

If you're into fishing along the Atlantic coast you might want to check out **Rudow's Guide to Fishing the Mid Atlantic**, a how-to/where-to book which includes over 300 hotspots detailed on 38 custom-marked charts, covering from North Carolina to New York. The book includes sections on coastal bay, inlet, inshore and offshore fishing, tackle and tactics, and covers each specific species of fish found in the region, from sea bass to swordfish.

IT'S AVAILABLE AT WWW.GETGUP.COM

RUDOW'S GUIDE TO

Fishing
the
Chesapeake

Lenny Rudow

Inveterate Chesapeake Bay anglers should be interested in Rudow's Guide to Fishing the Chesapeake, which examines every tributary and main-stem area of the bay from its headwaters to the CBBT in detail. Hotspots are meticulously detailed on custom-marked charts, and separate sections of the book cover bay-appropriate tackle and tactics.

IT'S AVAILABLE AT WWW.GETGUP.COM

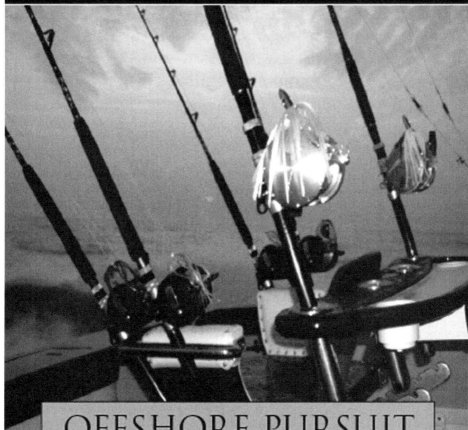

"John Unkart introduced me to a trolling rig I had never seen before, and the first day I tried it we hooked up with six bluefin tuna!" — Lenny Rudow, Boating Magazine's Ultimate Angler

OFFSHORE PURSUIT

BILLFISH · TUNA · WAHOO · MAHI-MAHI

OFFSHORE RIGGING AND TACTICS BY A PROFESSIONAL
WITH 40 YEARS OF EXPERIENCE

BY JOHN UNKART

Hard-core offshore enthusiasts need to take a peek at Offshore Pursuit, by John Unkart, a professional mate with over 40 years of blue-water experience. From rigging techniques to tips on how to fight trophy fish, everything you need to know to hunt pelagics is covered in this book. Best of all, Unkart's clear, concise writing style makes the most complex knots and involved tactics easy to understand. Whether you're a novice or an expert, you will become a better angler by reading Unkart's book.

IT'S AVAILABLE AT WWW.GETGUP.COM

TUNA FISHING

A MODERN APPROACH FROM THE COCKPIT UP

BY JON MEADE

[ALBACORE * BIGEYE * BLACKFIN * BLUEFIN * YELLOWFIN]

Tuna nuts will want to know about Tuna Fishing: A Modern Approach from the Cockpit Up, by Jon Meade. Capt. Mead—a noted tuna fishing authority who writes for publications including In The Bite, Sport Fishing, and Boating Magazine—grew up in the big game sport-fishing community and has worked boats from Ocean City to Palm Beach and beyond. His knowledge and expertise pours out on the pages of this book, which details cutting-edge tricks and techniques professional anglers use to win big-money tournaments and put meat in the box day in and day out. Want proof? No problem—Meade was running the cockpit of the Sea Wolf when the boat took the 181 pound yellowfin that took first place for tuna, and won a cool quarter-mil in the 2006 Mid Atlantic $500,000. He also was running the cockpit when this boat took an 875 pound bluefin tuna and a 210 pound big eye.

AND YES, IT'S AVAILABLE AT WWW.GETGUP.COM

Geared Up is dedicated to bringing saltwater anglers the how-to/where-to information that to date has been impossible to get without putting in years and years of fishing and networking among professional anglers. The books published by Geared Up are full of the tricks, tips and tactics that professional captains and serious anglers usually keep to themselves. Our goal is bringing you the real-world, no BS saltwater fishing information you just can't get anywhere else. If you want to read entertaining fishing stories, get Hemmingway. If you want hard-core how-to/where-to fishing information, get Geared Up. You can find Geared Up's books at our web site (www.getgup.com or www.geareduppublications.com) and in fine tackle shops and book stores. And, we offer the following guarantee: If these books don't help you catch more fish, we'll eat our bait!

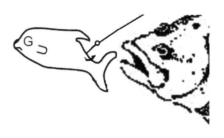

GEARED UP PUBLICATIONS, LLC
EDGEWATER, MD
WWW.GEAREDUPPUBLICATIONS.COM